MW01490976

# Multimodal Pedagogies in Diverse Classrooms

Pippa Stein's book deals with what is maybe the central issue among the vast, daunting problems of education for South Africa's post-apartheid society – the issue of 'literacy'. She shows the starkly desperate problems of so many children, their vibrant response, their energy and imagination, powerful and, often, filled with joy. Out of that she develops a theory around learning and making meaning for conditions of profound diversity, a theory that could only have been thought in South Africa; yet provides a path through there as much as here or anywhere.

Gunther Kress, Professor of Education, Head of School,
School of Culture, Language and Communication,
Centre for Multimodal Research, Institute of Education, London

*Multimodal Pedagogies in Diverse Classrooms* examines how the classroom can become a democratic space founded on the integration of different histories, modes of representation, feelings, languages and discourses, and is essential reading for anyone interested in the connection between multimodality, pedagogy, democracy and social justice in diverse classrooms.

Pippa Stein combines theory with material taken from post-apartheid classrooms in South Africa where students from different language and cultural backgrounds negotiate the ongoing tensions between tradition and modernity, Western and African intellectual thought, as well as the apartheid-past of their parents, and their own aspirations for the future. This insightful book argues that classrooms can become 'transformative' sites in which students can develop curricula and pedagogies which speak to the diversity of global societies, and looks at:

- How multimodality can be used to promote social justice and democracy in diverse classrooms;
- The forms of representation through which students make meaning in classrooms;
- How those forms contribute to the building of democratic cultures;
- The cultural resources available to students, and how they are used for learning;
- Difference as a productive energy for learning.

Dealing with issues such as democracy, politics of difference, diversity, multicultural and multilingual classrooms, this book is as pertinent to readers across the globe as it is to those in South Africa, and will be invaluable and fascinating reading for anyone working or interested in this field.

**Pippa Stein** is Associate Professor in language and literacy education at University of the Witwatersrand, Johannesburg, and head of the department of Applied English Language Studies.

# Multimodal Pedagogies in Diverse Classrooms

## Representation, rights and resources

Pippa Stein

LONDON AND NEW YORK

First published 2008 by Routledge
2 Park Square, Milton Park, Abingdon, Oxon OX14 4RN

Simultaneously published in the USA and Canada
by Taylor & Francis Inc.
711 Third Avenue, New York, NY 10017

*Routledge is an imprint of the Taylor & Francis Group, an informa business*

First issued in paperback 2012

© 2008 Pippa Stein

Typeset in Garamond 3 by
Florence Production Ltd, Stoodleigh, Devon

All rights reserved. No part of this book may be reprinted or reproduced or utilised in any form or by any electronic, mechanical, or other means, now known or hereafter invented, including photocopying and recording, or in any information storage or retrieval system, without permission in writing from the publishers.

*British Library Cataloguing in Publication Data*
A catalogue record for this book is available from the British Library

*Library of Congress Cataloging in Publication Data*
Stein, Pippa.
Multimodal pedagogies in diverse classrooms: representation, rights and resources/Pippa Stein.
p. cm.
Includes bibliographical references and index.
1. Multicultural education. 2. Critical pedagogy. I. Title.
LC1099.S736 2008
370.117 – dc22 2007020599

ISBN13: 978–0–415–54176–3 (pbk)
ISBN13: 978–0–415–40165–4 (hbk)
ISBN13: 978–0–203–93580–4 (ebk)

For my father and mother
Phillip and Shirley Stein

# Contents

# Illustrations

# Acknowledgements

This book has been many years in the making. It has been shaped by my experiences of working with children in and out of schools since the early 1980s. Making sense of the complexity of children's meaning-making in these varied contexts has been very challenging, and without help from numerous people, in South Africa and beyond, I could not have reached this point. My grateful thanks go to all of them.

This volume is a tribute to the creativity and resourcefulness of South African children, many of whom, 13 years after democracy, continue to live below the poverty line in circumstances of extreme hardship. My heartfelt thanks to the children whose voices are present in this text, and to all the children who gave of themselves with energy and enthusiasm in the narrative projects which are the focus of this book. I am indebted to the principals and teachers who allowed me access to their schools and classrooms, sharing their ideas and guiding me along the way. Many thanks to Pam Mdhluli, Fred Maphula, Colin Northmore, Ntsoake Senja, Tshidi Mamabolo and Charles Sambo. I owe a special acknowledgment to Martha Mokgoko and Ruth Mfhilo who taught me so much about working with children, and who graciously welcomed me into their homes.

This research would not have happened without the inspirational leadership of Gunther Kress who has been central to this project from the start. The book draws heavily on his theoretical work in multimodal social semiotics and literacy. From his exacting mentoring, powerful insights, encouragement and friendship, I have learnt new ways of writing and thinking.

My colleagues in Applied English Language Studies have been supportive and generous in every way: many thanks to Hilary Janks, Yvonne Reed, Stella Granville, Sue van Zyl, Pinky Makoe, Leila Kajee, Kerryn Dixon, Carolyn McKinney, Patricia Watson and Magauta Mphahlele.

A major theme of this book is how children creatively draw on a range of semiotic resources in their meaning making. I am profoundly indebted to my colleagues at the University of the Witwatersrand who have introduced me to the rich field of Southern African literary, literacy and cultural studies and who continue to guide my learning and reading in this area. I owe special thanks to Isabel Hofmeyr, Liz Gunner, Sarah Nuttall, Fiona Rankin-Smith, Karen Harber, Rayda Becker, Karel Nel, Michelle Adler, Robert Muponde, Jonathan Paton, Carolyn Hamilton, Achille Mbembe, David Coplan, Jon Hylsop, Hilary Janks, Michael Titlestad, Peter Delius, Susan Suzman and Susan Harrop-Allin. I have also learnt hugely from colleagues in education who work in social justice, pedagogy and curriculum: Lynne Slonimsky, Penny Enslin, Shirley Pendlebury and Emilia Potenza. Ruth Sack's deep knowledge of children's art-making has been invaluable. Arlene Archer and Lucia Thesen, from the University of Cape Town, have been wonderful fellow travellers in the unpredictable field of multimodality. Mastin Prinsloo and Carole Bloch, from the University of Cape Town, provided me with the opportunity to research children's literacy in the Children's Early Literacy Project (CELL) and, through this, deepened my understanding of the challenges children face to become literate in South Africa today. Patti Henderson has been a guiding light, always, through her work with children, and a most valued critical friend.

The Wits Multiliteracies Research Project was a highly stimulating space to explore aspects of visual communication, performance and writing. Working with Denise Newfield, David Andrew, Joni Brenner, Tshidi Mamabolo, Robert Maungedzo, Alison Beynon, Marion Drew and Kathleen Wemmer stretched my thinking around multimodality and multiliteracies in diverse contexts. Denise Newfield has been a pillar of support in every way – a friend, a colleague, an intellectual and writing partner whose insights and honesty I value enormously.

This work has benefitted from the perspectives and support of many colleagues beyond the Limpopo, who have given me opportunities to share this work with wider audiences. My grateful thanks to Brian Street, Carey Jewitt, Bonny Norton, Bill Cope, Mary Kalantzis, Kate Pahl, Jennifer Rowsell, Rimli Bhattacharya and Sneha Gupta. Carol Fox and Shirley Brice-Heath visited South Africa in 1994, shortly after the first democratic elections, and this study was influenced by our conversations on narrative during that momentous time in South African history.

This research could not have taken place without the help of particular individuals who acted as transcribers, translators, interviewers, 'cultural informants', guides and professional assistants. I owe an enormous debt to Patrick Baloyi who speaks eight South African languages, and to Thandiwe Mkhabela, Mogobe Mmaboko and Xoli Norman for their invaluable assistance as researchers and translators.

While the opinions and conclusions in this book are mine alone, numerous students in Applied English Language Studies have contributed to my thinking around the themes in this book. Many thanks to Florah Mohlala, Simon Zeray Abraham, Donald Masasanya, Natalie Lockhart, Barbara Baloyi, Lesley Emanuel, Toni Joosten, Alison Beynon, Lyn Meyer, Andrew Brouard, Deidre Alder, Elspeth Kempe, Paula Gains, Adele Piccolo, Aloysius Conduah and Belinda Mendelowitz.

This study was conducted over many years and financially supported in part by the National Research Foundation, The Spencer Foundation and the University of the Witwatersrand, Faculty of Humanities. It has been a great pleasure to work with the editorial and production team at Routledge and I wish to thank them all for their supportive and super-efficient production of this book.

I am deeply grateful to my extended family and friends, who sustained me with their love, through very difficult times: Liza, Patti, Fiona, Debbie, Ruth, Liz, Karen, Mark, Penny, Robbie, Rosie, Virginia, Dudu, Noleen, Donna, Dumi, my parents Phillip and Shirley and Benjamin, my son. And finally, my deepest thanks to Malcolm Purkey, for his passionate belief in this work, for his penetrating insights, for enduring love.

# Chapter 1

# A multimodal social semiotic approach

## Introduction

This book explores how language and literacy classrooms can become more democratic spaces through addressing a central issue in teaching, learning and its assessment: namely, *the forms of representation through which students make their meanings*. In this sense, the book is about the politics of representation and the politics of difference in diverse, multicultural and multilingual classrooms. It focuses attention on the forms of representation which are produced from the many cultural sources students have access to, and examines these resources for their meaning potential. To put it simply, this book examines the question: how can the classroom, as a multi-semiotic space, become a complex, democratic space, founded on the productive integration of diverse histories, modes, genres, epistemologies, feelings, languages and discourses?

Drawing on theories in the emerging field of multimodal communication from a social semiotic perspective, this book locates itself within a paradigm shift that is taking place in relation to conceptualising communication and representation in learning environments. Following the work of Kress (1995, 1997a, 2000a, 2003), Kress and van Leeuwen (1996, 2nd edn 2006, 2001) and van Leeuwen (2005), this shift has been described as *a multimodal approach* to representation and communication. In the field of literacy education, this approach has been variously referred to as 'multimodal literacy', 'multimodality' and 'multimodal social semiotics'. Traditional theories of communication are monomodal in their focus on how language communicates meaning. However, a multimodal theory of communication holds that meaning is made, always, in the many different modes and media which make up a communicational ensemble. A multimodal approach to teaching and learning characterises communication in classrooms beyond the linguistic: language, in speech and writing, is only one mode of communication among many. Other modes can include image, space, gesture, colour, sound and movement, all of which function to communicate meaning in an integrated, multilayered way. In a multimodal approach, all modes of communication drawn on in the making of meaning are given equally serious attention.

The shift from a focus on language to a focus on mode has resulted in a shift in the relevant theoretical fields, from the discipline of linguistics, which focuses on language, to semiotics, which studies signs and their meanings in all their different material realisations. The semiotic framework which this book draws on is *social semiotics*, signalling its emphasis on the social dimensions of how human beings represent their meanings in the concrete social world. Social semiotics fundamentally challenges the idea of closed, stable systems of representation in which human beings are users of systems, rather than active transformers of semiotic resources. Social semiotic theories place human beings at the centre of meaning–making: as designers and interpreters of meaning, they make active choices, according to their interests, from the semiotic resources available to them. Semiotic resources of representation are not fixed: they are fluid, constantly changing as human beings' representational needs change. Thus, from a social semiotic perspective, communication as sign production, 'reception' and transformation, can be understood as a product of how people work with, use and transform the semiotic resources available to them in specific moments of history, culture and power.

This shift from an emphasis on language to mode has far-reaching implications for education. As Kress *et al.* (2001, 2005) have demonstrated in Science and English classrooms, the idea that each mode provides teachers and students with a range of meaning–making potentials or 'affordances' has consequences for learning, the shaping of knowledge, the development of curriculum and its assessment practices. It has implications for students' identities and how cultures and identities are shaped in learning environments. This shift has important implications for thinking about pedagogy: if all pedagogic processes, including the designing of teaching and learning materials, are understood as the selection and configuration of the multimodal resources available in the classroom, then pedagogical processes can be viewed as complex signs of what it is that the producers of this sign 'needed to' or 'chose to say' at that particular moment. The producers of these signs may include the state, national curriculum designers, schools and their boards, parents, school subject departments, individual teachers and students. Such processes of sign-making are never neutral, however. They are invested with unequal power relations, resource constraints and forms of coercion and resistance operating among different interest groups in the educational policy-practice nexus (Bhattacharya *et al.* 2007). For example, in South Africa, how HIV/AIDS education is mainstreamed in the school curriculum is an area of fraught debate and controversy which gets 'actualised' by individual schools and teachers in a myriad of ways. Any investigation, at the micro level, into how it is taken up and enacted in classrooms by teachers and students has to be read against the macro socio-political context of tension between denial, silence and stigmatisation of the disease, and open acknowledgement and action focused on treatment and prevention.

This book shows how a multimodal semiotic approach can be applied to educational practice to enhance learning in contexts of diversity and difference. As such, it takes a critical perspective (Freire 1970; Mclaren 1989; Giroux 1992; Luke 2004; Norton and Tooney 2004) in relation to multimodal semiotics, arguing that classrooms have the potential to become 'transformative' sites in which students' representational resources can be used productively and critically to develop curricula and pedagogies which speak to the diversity of global societies and the development of students' voices. It links the building of democratic culture specifically to the forms through which students are permitted to make their meanings. In mainstream classrooms, certain forms of representation are dominant and valued, like standard forms of written language. Students who do not perform 'to standard', for whatever reasons, are labelled as 'deficient'. In this book, I challenge the idea of the dominance of a single form of representation. Rather, I explore how different knowledges and cultural forms can be represented through multiple forms of representation, how these diverse forms can be 'remixed', rubbed up against each other to create new forms, new meanings and new possibilities for learning, what Millard (2006) calls 'fusion' pedagogies. This is not to deny students access to dominant discourses of power, but to reconceptualise teaching and learning as holding in creative tension access to dominant discourses, while building on the rich variety of resources that students bring to learning contexts. Such pedagogies can be harnessed for establishing classroom cultures in which social and cultural difference is valued positively, as a resource, not as an obstacle.

These issues are addressed through examples from South Africa in the post-apartheid transformation period (1994 to present). South Africa is presented as a high instance of a democracy in formation, as a whole society engages with what it means to move from a colonial history and deeply racialised, officially segregated white minority-controlled state to a modern African capitalist democracy founded on constitutional rights, equity, reconciliation, redress and inclusivity. The examples in this book have been selected mainly from projects in narrative in language and literacy classrooms, where students from different language and cultural backgrounds negotiate ongoing tensions in the society between 'tradition' and 'modernity', between Western and African forms of intellectual thought, consciousness and culture, between local African languages and English, between indigenous, local knowledges and new information technologies, between schooled learning and out-of-school knowledge, between the apartheid-past of their parents and their own aspirations for the future.

## Three stories

### *1980s*

This research began in the 1980s during the last decade of apartheid rule in South Africa, when I started working as an English teacher with young children and teachers in Soweto, then a segregated township for black people on the outskirts of Johannesburg. I was concerned at that point with the stark contrasts between the children's worlds inside the classroom, and what they were witnessing and experiencing outside the classroom. Inside the classroom, where they were learning English as an additional language, they were chanting textbook drill and pattern practice of English grammatical forms, answering questions in variations of controlled composition, and reading strange colonial texts about African children living in remote rural villages. This was going on whilst all around, an urban political war was being waged: the apartheid army was patrolling the streets in *casspirs* (armoured vehicles), high–school children were being shot and tortured, buildings were being burnt and school boycotts called. I wondered where children were being given the opportunity to connect learning in classrooms with their everyday lives. At the same time, I was constantly hearing racist, deficit remarks in (white) educational circles concerning the linguistic, creative and cognitive abilities of black children.

As a response to these views, and with a deepening sense of the lack of connection between children's home lives and school lives, a colleague, Martha Mokgoko, and I started running afternoon classes in a local community centre in Soweto with groups of young children. We called our group *SPEAK*. We were working in an intensely stressful political situation of violence and brutality. The day we started our classes, the government declared a state of emergency. Troops patrolled the streets and the army was invading schools. We constituted these classes as 'unpoliced zones' where children could explore and represent their worlds in playful, imaginative and uncensored ways that combined multiple discourses and modes of representation. It was in that space that it became clear the extent to which children's daily experiences in classrooms were constraining and denying them opportunities to flourish as fully expressive human beings. In denying these children the capacity for voice, schools were functioning as another arm of apartheid surveillance and control.

Many of the roots of my interest in innovative or 'alternative' pedagogies grew out of a political response to the teaching situation in which we found ourselves: the media were severely restricted by the emergency regulations and any reports of 'unrest' or political resistance in any of the black townships were heavily censored. Two guiding principles formed the core of our language learning and teaching approach: what we called 'a genuine search for meaning' within 'an atmosphere of freedom and learner responsibility' in which children were encouraged to listen to each other and respect each other's rights to different opinions. Teachers were encouraged to listen to and respect the opinions of children. This mutual respect was hard to engender in South Africa, where, historically, there has been no tradition of religious, racial or political tolerance.

It seemed clear to us that any language pedagogy which had as its core aim 'a genuine search for meaning' had to start with children's lives and daily experiences in some form of critical engagement. A primary aim was to develop children's 'voices'. As such, this pedagogy was deeply influenced by Freire's critical pedagogy (1970; Freire and Macedo 1987) which had already impacted on several of the progressive adult education programmes in South Africa at the time. We wanted to promote a culture of talking rather than fighting and help children to reflect critically on the social and material conditions of their lives so they could understand the root causes of the violence they were witnessing and experiencing. At the time, this 'culture of talking' was developed in and through one language – English – because I was committed at that time to working in an 'English as the target language' teaching model. Since then I have changed my views: developing a 'culture of talking' means working with all the language resources that children have access to. In Gauteng, where I live and work, most children are multilingual, drawing on several African languages in their communicative repertoires.

Language was not the only mode of communication, however. Because children had different levels of access to English, and talking was potentially dangerous, there were many instances where they wanted to tell their stories through dance, music and performance, with no watertight divisions between them. Drawing became a more direct way of showing what was difficult to describe. These sessions became known as 'Behind the Headlines' because in a very real sense, most of the experiences witnessed or reported on were suppressed in the national media. These multimodal texts then became the primary texts around which discussion and critical reflection would happen. Figure 1.1 is an example of drawing and writing by SPEAK children in the late 1980s about a notorious incident when youth from the liberation movement, the African National Congress (ANC), were forcing people to boycott shops in the city and to stop using state-owned transport in the form of buses. Those who defied this boycott were forced by ANC youth 'comrades' to drink fish oil or soap powder on their return from these shops. Buses were being burnt at the same time.

Drama was used extensively to explore current themes and events. Martha Mokgoko made a play with the children based on the true story of one of the children, a 12-year-old Soweto boy, whose father had saved up to buy him a bicycle for his birthday. One afternoon, three thieves robbed him of his bicycle at gunpoint. Frank's older brother went looking for the thieves and found one of them. He called his father and they both assaulted the thief, took him to the police who released him without charges. Frank never reclaimed his bicycle. The play ended with a poem by the children, pleading for joint community action against the high levels of violence and crime in Soweto. Apartheid was cited as one of the major causes of this crime rate. Here Martha Mokgoko describes the process of making this story into a play, *Frank's Bicycle*:

In this picture the woman is drinking fish oil.The shops are burning.We see dogs and a burning bus. People are not supposed to drink fish oil because they will get a disease. It seems that this woman was forced to drink fish oil because when the comrades said we must not buy in town she became stubborn and bought groceries in town.It is very clear that if people drink fish oil they will suffer and die. We suggest that people must not burn shops and buses because we cannot travel easily. We suggest that we must not burn shops because we need food.We cannot live without food.

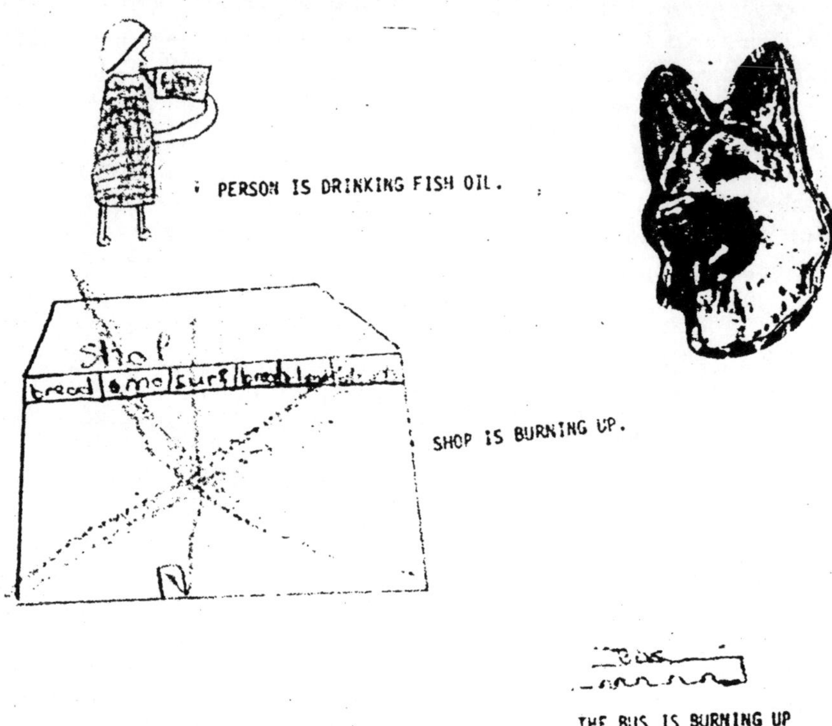


*Figure 1.1* SPEAK children's drawings and writing

At the time, the children were undergoing political strain. It was tense in the class. I decided that we should talk about the daily events and as we talked, many stories emerged. As we discussed these stories, the children began to relax. For some problems, they didn't have solutions but through discussion, we came up with solutions. We laughed too, about very serious things. We heard each other's stories and we negotiated

> which one to use for the play. It was painful . . . you found there was agreement and disagreement amongst the children, but we wanted to encourage debate, not fighting. We then had a series of workshops on Frank's story to make the script. The whole process was very communicative. For example, in order to find the thief, Frank's brother had to give a perfect description of him. For this scene we gave each child in the class an opportunity to describe the thief in a creative way. Frank would then decide if the description was true. This became very comic. The children learnt a lot from this process. They learnt how to observe carefully, how to investigate, what kinds of questions to ask a thief . . . It also gave them a chance to reflect on a situation. This person was beaten up but we don't encourage this kind of violence. At the end of the day, you are building the children; you are educating the whole person for the future. These children are our future leaders. Next time Frank meets a problem like this, he will say, halt. We must act collectively and the violence will stop. We are asking people to think, not just to use their feelings. We also want them to be creative in English – to make a play and write a poem from this experience.
>
> (Stein 1993: 15)

At a certain point into the project, we asked the children what they wanted to talk and read about. A frequent request was for 'our history'. In state schools at the time, the only history taught was South African history from a white apartheid perspective. In response to this request, we set up an oral history project on a local mixed race neighbourhood, called Sophiatown, from which communities were forcibly removed by the state in the 1950s. Students compiled their own life histories and brought their parents in to recount their histories. One child's great grandfather refused to be interviewed because he did not want to recall the bitterness of the past. Teachers on the project used these stories as one way of helping children to talk about what was happening to them in what became increasingly a kind of therapy.

The teaching and learning approach in SPEAK was an attempt to mesh a critical pedagogy with the dominant English Language Teaching (ELT) paradigm of the 1980s (Brumfit and Johnson 1979) during the early days of communicative language teaching. We were very influenced by Harmer's (1983) model of communicative language teaching in its emphasis on developing fluency and accuracy tasks within 'authentic communicative contexts'. However, what counted as meaningful in the communicative language teaching paradigm – pair and group work, functional uses of English in 'real world' contexts in the cities of London and New York – was far removed from the context of the armed struggle being played out in the burning streets of South African townships. Our experience of the social crisis in South Africa did not seem to fit with the bland 'neutrality' of the mainstream ELT models being applied internationally.

## 1994

In April 1994, the first democratic elections in South African history took place, and Nelson Mandela was inaugurated as the first black president. This year marked the beginning of a new era in South African history with a negotiated settlement which led to the dismantling of apartheid structures, and the transfer of power from a white elite minority to black majority rule within a modern democratic state. As the old apartheid order heaved and cracked, making way for the new, the word ringing in our ears and on the streets was *transformation*.

During this year, I worked on a storytelling project with a class of Grade 7 teenagers in a township school on the East Rand, east of Johannesburg. The majority of students were multilingual and communicatively competent in a mixture of at least three South African indigenous languages, with English as an additional language. Drawing on the students' oral storytelling resources, I asked them to think of any stories from their families or community networks that they would like to share with the class. Out of 37 students, three volunteered. A colleague, Patrick Baloyi, who speaks eight South African languages, set the ball rolling by telling some stories his father told him when he was growing up in a village in Venda. He told these stories in Tswana, his home language. This warmed up the audience. They started showing signs of interest. We then asked the students: Tell any stories *in the language/s it was told to you*. This shift from using only English to using any language as a resource initially disturbed the students – it was out of their sense of the ordinary. A sign up at the back of the class, 'You must speak English at school' watched over them. However, after some prompting and assurances that they would not be punished, the students took the risk.

What began as a fairly loose, unstructured language activity was transformed over the year into a sustained project in narrative across multiple semiotic modes in which students drew heavily on cultural forms and resources familiar to them. By the end of the year, the students had produced over 100 stories in eight South African languages, in speech, writing, image and multimodal performance. Recordings of all the students' performances were made on video and shown to the students and teachers. I began analysing the stories from a sociolinguistic perspective, looking at features of code-switching and mixing. However it soon became apparent to me that what I was interested in analysing – the 'language' of their stories from a linguistic perspective – did not do justice to what was actually happening in the classroom in relation to the rich context of live performance in which these stories were embedded. In linguistic theory, all aspects of communication that do not involve the linguistic are clustered under the term 'paralinguistic features', including the use of voice, gesture and body 'language'. However, in these students' performances, the use of voice, rhythm, melody, eye contact, facial expressions and body movement was as important to the production of meaning as language. I could not be blind to the students' use of special click sounds, hip movements, intonation patterns and interactions with the audience in which the performers and audiences were engaged in a relationship of mutual pleasure and delight, in which imaginations were set free. It was clear to me that the particular performances styles were deeply familiar, rooted in the children's everyday lives and that these formed part of broader histories of communicative practices integral to their social and cultural worlds beyond the classroom.

These storytelling practices which drew on urban multilingualism, elaborated gestures and sounds combined with the visuals of performance, demanded a new theoretical lens, a new body of theory. Shifting from a focus on language alone to a focus on communicative resources and practices, I began to look at how the students were drawing on multi-semiotic representational resources to transform meanings within specific communicative practices. I became interested in different modes of communication, in the cultural resources students were recruiting from their homes, streets, schools, communities and contemporary media to shape meaning.

## 2006

In 2006, Charles Sambo, an English teacher from a Soweto high school, was approached by his Grade 11 students seeking his guidance. Most of the students live in the informal settlements or 'shacks' near the school. His students were angry. They wanted to know how they could go about campaigning for improved service delivery from local government. They wanted running water, sanitation, electricity and regular trash removal – all denied to them because they live in shacks. Sambo, whose 'starting point was hope', agreed to help them develop the skills they needed to voice their complaints in a reasoned and principled way. To begin, he asked them to represent their own personal experiences of *Shack Life* from multiple perspectives, using any semiotic resources they had access to. The students borrowed cameras and took photos of their homes and surrounding areas. They produced oral poetry which they performed in class. They wrote lively texts about their experiences of living in what they called 'sqwata camps'. Their teacher showed them how to write formal letters of complaint to the municipality, how to write reports on their living conditions for submission to local councillors. He taught them how to draw up a manifesto. Finally, he worked with them on how to make their voices heard in a number of different sites, including the Internet. In this project which draws on critical, multimodal pedagogy, Sambo worked responsively and creatively with students' inner and outer worlds, building on their expressed desire to connect what they learn in school to improving the conditions of their lives. Through working with a range of emotional registers, epistemologies, genres and modes, Sambo has enabled his students to build their capacities for voice.

Hopefully, processes such as these can advance their long term interests in relation to social justice and poverty alleviation.

## What this book is about

These three stories provide a backdrop to the issues explored in this book in relation to the tension between children's creativity and capacity for meaning-making which builds on their everyday worlds, and the limits, denials and silences imposed on these capacities in classroom spaces. This is especially the case for poor children who live on the margins of this society and who do not have access to the cultural capital and networking strategies of the privileged classes. I frame this tension as an issue of children's 'rights to representation', along with socioeconomic and human rights.

This book attempts to answer two separate questions related to these issues. One is about children's multimodal meaning-making: *How do children draw on multi-semiotic, multimodal cultural resources in their meaning-making?* The second question concerns pedagogy in diverse classrooms: *What kinds of pedagogies support learning in contexts of diversity?* I have linked the two questions by suggesting that the second question can be addressed by answering the first. In other words, investigating how children engage with the meaning-making potentials of modes, for which purposes and for what effects, can provide valuable insights into their socio-cultural worlds, knowledges and identities. Through developing a deeper, more systematic understanding of how multimodality is articulated materially in children's texts as 'signs' of learning we can begin to consider the implications for the classroom and refine our pedagogical processes to improve learning in contexts of diversity. As the UK Literacy Association (UKLA) and Qualifications and Curriculum Authority (QCA) researchers note in their booklets *More than Words:1 and 2* we need to know how to describe what children know and can do as shown in their multimodal texts so that teachers help pupils develop and extend their control of different modes. It also helps us to understand how we can help students 'to get better at multimodality' (UKLA/QCA 2004, 2005)

In order to address these two questions, the book analyses a range of children's multimodal texts, using a multimodal social semiotic approach in combination with a number of other theoretical orientations. This interdisciplinary perspective includes New Literacy Studies, Southern African cultural studies and studies on childhood and children's rights in South Africa. These theories and perspectives are presented in Chapter 2, followed by case study discussions of children's multimodal meaning-making from a range of sites. These studies form the basis on which a concept of multimodal pedagogies is explored in Chapter 6, where four instances of multimodal pedagogies as classroom practice engage with the concept of multimodality for different purposes and in different ways.

## Research methodology

Trying to find out more about how children engage with meaning-making in classrooms demands particular approaches to the kinds of data needed, how this data is collected and how it is analysed. There are different ways of getting at 'how', all of them dependent on particular theories of meaning-making. In this book, meaning-making is understood as a multi-semiotic, material social practice in which the children as 'sign-makers' recruit the semiotic resources they need in order to communicate. A textual product is understood to be a material form in which multimodality is realised. To this end, in a multimodal social semiotic approach, students' multimodal texts constitute one form of data. They are forms of classroom 'materials' which are treated as semiotic objects or 'signs' that bear 'concrete traces' of the cognitive and affective work involved in their production (Kress *et al.* 2001: 38).

However, in order to gain a more in-depth understanding of how these multimodal texts form part of children's cultural histories and communicative practices in their everyday lives, this study draws on elements of an ethnographic-style approach to educational research. An ethnographic approach, in different variations, is central to the ways in which New Literacy Studies (Heath 1983; Street 1984, 1993, 2001, 2005; Barton and Hamilton 1998) researches literacy as a social practice, using participant–observation, interviews and fieldwork methods to investigate how people's ideas and everyday practices shape the cultural use of literacy in their local communities and contexts. This approach to literacy attempts to understand and make visible the meanings that people attach to literacy and how literacy texts fit into the practices of their everyday lives.

In this study, I work with multimodal social semiotics and New Literacy Studies as complementary frameworks for analysing learners' communicative practices in classrooms. The ethnographic data adds important ethical and interpretive dimensions to the micro-analysis of students' multimodal texts, enabling the researcher to situate the communicative practice within larger frames of meaning which make sense to the participants themselves and throw different perspectives on the notion of the sign-maker's 'interests' in the moment of interaction. Such interests arise out of the maker's own social histories, social locations and awareness of the context of addressivity in which the sign is being made.

Pahl and Rowsell (2006) in *Travel Notes from the New Literacy Studies* bring together New Literacy Studies and multimodality in an attempt to merge 'a social practice account of literacy *with* a description of communication systems' (2006: 1). They see 'identity and social practice in the materiality of texts' and argue that ethnographic methods enable researchers to 'trace practices in texts':

> It is not enough to analyse texts as single, isolated entities since such a system does not account for the problematic of meaning and the embodied meanings that lie within texts, which instantiate facets of an author's identity in practice.
>
> (Pahl and Rowsell 2006: 2)

## The data

The explorations into children's meaning-making in this book are based on a number of research projects which span more than a decade. The main body of data comes from two school-based projects in narrative and story-telling. The first project, 'The Spruitview Storytelling Project', was carried out with Grade 7 children in a co-ed primary school east of Johannesburg. This year-long project, which I ran with one class for one and a half hours per week during school time, took place during 1994. The data set from this project consists of the students' multimodal narrative texts – drawings, videotaped performances and writings – which were produced in response to specific pedagogical tasks. Selected data from this data-set forms the basis of the case study discussions in Chapters 3 and 4.

The second project called 'The Olifantsvlei "Fresh Stories" Project', was undertaken in 2001 with Grades 1 and 2 children by a group of early literacy teachers in a semi-rural primary school west of Johannesburg. This school provides for children who live in poverty in nearby informal settlements or 'shacks'. The focus of this project was a three-month literacy project on developing 'fresh stories' – new, original stories created by the children in multiple languages. It involved teachers and children in a series of sequenced, creative activities in narrative which worked across semiotic modes. The data collected from these classes consisted of drawings, 3D sculptural figures, audiotaped monologues, writings and videotaped performances, supplemented by classroom observations, focus groups discussions and individual interviews with children and teachers. Data from this project forms the basis of the discussion in Chapter 5.

In Chapter 6, four examples of multimodal pedagogies implemented in 2006 and 2007 are discussed. Two examples are based on the research of colleagues Marion Drew, Kathleen Wemmer and Susan Harrop-Allin, all of whom are researching in the field of multimodality and pedagogy. The two other examples are based on the work of secondary school English teachers, Colin Northmore and Charles Sambo, who have been exploring interesting ways of working with multimodal pedagogies in their schools in interesting ways. The data for these discussions are based on their students' multimodal textual products, interviews with the teachers and students' reflective comments on these projects.

## Data collection

The data was collected using a variety of methods. Classroom observation was central to both storytelling projects, but from different perspectives. In the Spruitview Storytelling Project, I was in the complicated role of both teacher and researcher. In the Olifantsvlei 'Fresh Stories' Project, I was in a more distant role as the researcher, observing other teachers. In the examples of multimodal pedagogies described in Chapter 6, in my role as researcher, I watched videotapes of the students' musical games, read the students' workbook on *Shack Life*, and interviewed the teachers on their procedures and practices. I also read descriptive and analytical accounts by teachers and researchers of what had occurred.

Since a multimodal social semiotic analysis is interested in the characteristics of multimodal texts as social signs, the careful collection of texts is central to this methodology. It also means that a large quantity of data can be accumulated. In the Spruitview and Olifantsvlei storytelling projects, all the students' texts in different modes were collected: these included their written stories in several South African languages, their 2D drawings on paper, their 3D sculptural figures, their spoken monologues or dialogues, and their live storytelling performances combining music, dance and theatre. These performances were recorded on one video camera, placed at the back of the classroom. As such, the video recordings of the performances are themselves positioned and selective: they are representations of the performances, shaped by the technologies of the video camera and the camera operator who made the video recording. Field notes made by the researcher complement the video recordings in an attempt to capture what else is going on during the live performance. The complexity of the transcription and analytic process in relation to the performance data is discussed in Chapter 3.

Interviews were conducted with students and teachers to gather more information about pedagogies and processes of making. Students were interviewed in pairs or focus groups either at break time or after school. A translator was always present to translate questions in English into African languages and vice versa. In many cases the translator was a child. These interviews and conversations always arose out of specific lessons or in response to particular stories. The discussions focused on the children's understandings of their stories, their reflections on the pedagogies that were being used and their multilingual language practices. Children were invited to talk about their processes of meaning-making and what the objects they were making meant to them. Some children were asked to comment on how their multi-semiotic texts formed part of histories of representation within their families and communities. These focus group discussions form part of the ethnographic-style fieldwork methods used in this study to understand how the children themselves, as participants, understood their own processes of representation within wider contexts of the cultural and communicative practices of their homes and communities.

A number of individual interviews were conducted with specific children whose texts are focused on in some depth. The purpose of these interviews was to gather more information about their processes of making, and the meanings they attributed to what they had made. For example, in Chapter 4, which describes the project in narrative, I interviewed all the children who had made 3D child/doll figures about the history of their 3D figures, where they had found the resources to make them, and how they might use these objects in their everyday lives and play. In the Spruitview Project, I interviewed Lungile, the young girl who is the focus of Chapter 3. I conducted these interviews with the help of a teacher as translator.

## Reflexivity, power and the research relationship

Each text we make is a complex sign reflecting our interests: in this sense, this study can be interpreted as a sign which reflects my own history and interests. The feminist research enterprise has drawn serious attention to the need for reflexivity in relation to the nature of research, the definition of and relationship with those with whom research is done, the characteristics and location of the researcher, and the creation and presentation of knowledges created in the research (Oleson 2000: 217). Collins (1990) and other black women feminists (hooks 1990; Anzaldua 1990) have challenged the 'whiteness' of much feminist research, contributing to a growing awareness of the importance of acknowledging the positionality or stance of the researcher within the research context. This perspective emphasises the extent to which the production of knowledge is intertwined with the complexities of the structural and power relations which occur between the researcher and the participants in the research process. These power relations operate at numerous levels including race, class, gender, age and sexual orientation, and are influenced by other important factors such as feelings and subjective judgements in relation to the particular research moment and context.

Teacher-research projects, such as the Spruitview Storytelling Project, in which a teacher researches her own practice, are fraught with issues around power and control in relation to the research participants. Power relations between teachers and students are structurally asymmetrical. Teachers are structurally in positions of power and clear hierarchies of authority are sustained through different forms of discipline and punishment. The students were not in any real position to resist or challenge the existing power relations, which gave me the power to demand of them some kind of response to the task which I was setting. Their parents, the school principal and their teachers had consented to their participation and, indeed, expected them to perform of their best in the situation. This fact means that the work that they produced was created within the institutional environment and not 'freely' produced in an informal, out of school environment, in which the students themselves may have had more control.

My structural position of power and authority as a teacher was compounded by race, gender, class and language factors. I was a 'white' woman teacher, working in a school where all the students (boys and girls) were 'black', and the teachers, mostly women, were black. In terms of the history of black and white power relations in South Africa, I was part of the ruling white minority at the time. The race relations were complex because of the 1994 historical moment of transition in which the ruling apartheid regime was ceding power to black majority rule. I was a teacher from Wits University, which is regarded as a prestigious institution among township youth. The fact that I spoke English, the medium of instruction and the language of prestige and power in South Africa, added to my position of power in this environment, as well as the fact that the children would be taught by a 'native' English speaker. All these factors influenced the research process in predictable and unexpected ways. Students did not challenge my authority, carrying out the tasks I asked them to do with some diligence and commitment. However, my status as an outsider and the pedagogical style I used which encouraged playfulness and a measure of freedom to express themselves in the languages and discourses they wished, influenced the kinds of texts they began to produce. This freedom was possible to some extent because I was an outsider, was not following the mainstream curriculum, nor was I assessing their work in any formal way.

One important area in which students exercised their power was in the area of their multilingual resources which they drew on throughout the project in ways that excluded me and constituted me as 'other'. I was a foreigner in a multilingual speech community in which 'my' language (English) was rarely used. The idea of translating from African languages into English and vice versa became a regular communicative practice in this class. There were numerous instances where I had to stop the class to ask them to 'translate' or 'explain' why they were all laughing. The students acted as cultural and linguistic brokers to help me to gain entry into their worlds. At the end of the year, in our reflections together on the process, a student asked me what I had felt as a 'linguistically disadvantaged person' in their class. I was touched by the sensitivity and concern of the question and interested in how the question showed their recognition of themselves as linguistically advantaged.

All the research described in this book, in which I have participated either as a teacher or researcher, has been influenced by my subject position of privilege – as a white, English speaking, middle class, woman academic. This has influenced, in subtle ways, how children have reacted or responded to my presence in class, and has shaped how teachers have worked with me. The classrooms have became micro-sites for issues of language, history, race, gender, canonicity and culture to be asserted, contested and negotiated. In a recent visit to a school in Soweto, where a teacher and I were working together on a creative project, as I was leaving the school, the teacher turned to me and said, 'Thank you for coming, now my status at this school will improve.' In view of this, it is important to bear in mind that this research and the interpretations which accompany it cannot be divorced from the larger social and political landscape in South Africa of which I am part.

## Researching children: some methodological and ethical considerations

Doing research with children raises concerns in relation to issues of power around access, consent, privacy and confidentiality, feedback, and transparency around the research process. Although these issues are not unique to researching children, they present researchers with challenges concerning the unequal power relations which exist between adults, researchers and child participants. A key differential in these relationships is age.

On the methodological aspects of collecting data from children, Mauthner argues for a child-centred approach to data collection which 'views children as subjects rather than objects of research' (Mauthner 1997: 17). A child-centred approach to data collection ensures that children are involved and consulted in the research process. This can occur in very practical ways through explaining the research topic to children in ways which they can understand, even though this itself is acknowledged as being highly challenging. It also involves negotiating consent from authority figures such as parents and guardians. Once access is gained, issues of interview privacy or a 'safe space' in which to interview is important, although there may be different cultural perspectives on 'privacy'. In the research literature on the unequal power relations between adults and children, children's rights become an issue. In an attempt to think about ways to equalise 'power relationships' between researcher and child, researchers have suggested a focus on reflexivity, flexibility, responsiveness and open-endedness in relation to research goals and methods. Children should be allowed to set their own agenda and talk about their own concerns and lives; in this way, they are foregrounding their subjective experiences. Another way to enable children to talk about their experiences and lives is to encourage them to tell stories and do drawings. These narratives provide children with 'their own voice' in the interviews. Children can be asked to reflect on their subjective experiences of the research process within small groups.

Multimodal research often involves video data, as video recording is the most efficient and effective means of capturing the different semiotic layers (full body movement, action, gesture, body position, talk, silence, interactions, use of space) in a communicative event. Although changing participants' names and protecting their identities is standard research practice, video data presents its own difficulties, particularly in relation to children who are vulnerable in this regard, and who need to be protected. Flewitt (2006) has stressed the importance of the researcher making considered, ethical judgements, in consultation with adult guardians about what visual images are essential to show. Digital technology has made it possible to protect identities by 'fuzzing' the faces of participants or reducing the pixel count. In the case of the research in this book, a selection of video stills from a storytelling performance is shown in Chapter 3.

Working with children becomes even more complicated in contexts of 'difference' where representing the research subjects, their stories, lives and practices, within a framework which is ethical and responsible both to them and to the research itself, is an ongoing challenge to the researcher and the research project. Behar has commented on how researchers 'ask for revelations from others' but 'we reveal little or nothing of ourselves; we make others vulnerable but we ourselves remain invulnerable' (Behar 1994: 273). These questions are very challenging and potentially threatening to any research process which involves the exploration of difference. They are particularly pertinent in post-colonial contexts where issues of difference and power are central to the politics of everyday life. Who speaks for whom? In whose voices should the stories be told? Who benefits from the telling? There are no simple answers to these questions in South Africa, with its history of racism and exploitation. However, it is clear that an important defining feature of research in this context is the way it takes seriously into account issues about ethics and research accountability. It also means being extra-sensitive to the possibilities of absences and silences in the data, which may come about due to cultural, linguistic, gender and racial differences.

## Research and social justice

Qualitative research is more than an inquiry project. It is also a 'moral, ethical and therapeutic project' (Denzin and Lincoln 2000: xvi). In drawing attention to children's texts and practices of meaning-making which are excluded, unrecognised or marginalised in local classrooms, this research project is committed to a social justice agenda concerning children and the politics of representation in local classrooms. In a country emerging out of a racist past where African children were systematically neglected, abused and denied basic human rights, it is important to raise the status of children and children's rights in the public sphere. This research contributes to this broad project by providing evidence of the complexity and variety of children's meaning-making. Through making visible children's creativity, social and cultural sensitivity, and resourcefulness in conditions of childhood adversity, it hopes to challenge dominant, deficit views concerning children's intelligence, creativity and resourcefulness, particularly those from poor families. In its investigation into ways of working with children's representational resources in culturally diverse pedagogic environments, this study critiques the narrowness of dominant models around what counts as acceptable languages, discourses, genres and modes of representation in mainstream classrooms. Such models deny local identities, experiences, languages and communicative practices. If South Africans are to make genuine advances in building a democratic culture in a post-colonial, post-apartheid period of reconciliation and development, it is necessary to acknowledge issues of difference and to use diversity creatively and energetically for the benefit of all. However, issues of difference also need to acknowledge the enormous disparities of wealth and poverty in South Africa. One has to creatively intervene in the contexts of poverty without either romanticising that poverty or embracing it as a necessary condition for creative advance.

## The organisation of this book

This book combines theoretical perspectives on multimodality with classroom applications. A major part of the book is devoted to the discussion and analysis of a range of South African children's multimodal texts produced in language and literacy classrooms. Multilingualism is an important component of these classes, where children have language repertoires which include local African languages and English.

Analysing multimodal texts produced by learners is a challenging, time-consuming activity. However, in order to teach children how to create and improve their multimodal texts, teachers need to have an understanding of what multimodality is, and how to apply key concepts to interpreting children's multimodal textual products. The purpose of Chapter 2 is to explain the overarching conceptual framework I developed in order to be able to analyse the multiple ways in which children were drawing on cultural resources in their meaning-making. This framework includes key ideas in multimodal social semiotics, New Literacy Studies, Southern African cultural studies and childhood and children's rights. The intention of the analytical chapters that follow – Chapters 3, 4 and 5 – is to demonstrate the application of this framework to a range of children's narrative texts spanning writing, spoken language, drawing, 3D artefacts and multimodal performance. These texts were all produced in two classroom projects focused on story. In both instances, the children's texts are contextualised within the multimodal pedagogies that produced them. In Chapter 6, the focus is on exploring pedagogy and multimodality. A definition of multimodal pedagogies is provided, followed by a description and analysis of four instances, from real classrooms, of teachers' use of multimodal pedagogies across the curriculum. These include Information and Communication Technology (ICT) and English, music education and audiology.

Finally, Chapter 7 focuses on the implications of the ideas raised in this book for developing classrooms as hybrid, democratic spaces which value diversity and difference. Developing multimodal assessment tools is central to this project. The chapter concludes with suggestions for teacher education in relation to multimodality and pedagogy.

# Chapter 2

# Multimodal analysis

## An interdisciplinary framework

### Introduction

This book takes a multimodal perspective on teaching and learning. It explores the potential of teaching and learning environments to become more democratic, inclusive spaces through investigating the meaning potential in the cultural and material sources to which children have access, to use and transform to make their meanings. Through examining real classrooms, where, every day, children and their teachers are engaged in 'the work of representation and discourse-making, of culture and development, of capital, communication and exchange' (Luke 2005), I argue that the forms of representation through which students make their meanings are signs which inflect what their makers 'wanted to say' at that particular moment. These signs are not neutral: they are traces of social practice, constantly moving and changing, as they move within ever-expanding 'webs of significance' (Pahl and Rowsell 2006: 8). As such, these signs can be viewed as complex inflections of the micro-sites in which they are embedded and broader, macro contexts of history and culture.

This is an interdisciplinary study. In order to have an informed perspective on children's multimodal sign-making practices within larger contexts of history and culture, it has been necessary to bring together a number of theoretical frameworks and fields of enquiry. I see these fields as complementary. They consist of: multimodal social semiotics, New Literacy Studies, Southern African cultural studies and South African childhood studies, focusing on children's rights and democracy. This chapter focuses on key ideas and assumptions in these fields which are pertinent to this research.

### Multimodal social semiotics

The term 'multimodality' in literacy education is mainly associated with social semiotic theory, referred to in the literature as 'multimodal social semiotics', 'multimodal literacy' and 'a multimodal social semiotic approach'. Multimodal social semiotics works with certain foundational assumptions in social semiotic theory. What follows is a brief introduction to these key ideas in social semiotics, followed by a focus on the concept of mode in multimodal social semiotics. It is important to stress that whereas the theoretical domain of multimodality is developing, multimodality is a new, emerging field and 'there is no orthodoxy' (Jewitt and Kress 2003).

Social semiotic theory is concerned with signs, sign-makers and sign-making. Social semiotics is based on a social semiotic account of language developed by Halliday (1978), in which meaning-making is conceptualised as choice from a range of interlocking options. Halliday argued that the grammar of a language is not a set of rules but 'a resource for making meanings' (1978: 192). This linguistic theory was the basis on which Hodge and Kress (1988) developed their theory of social semiotics which was interested in accounting for the different ways in which human beings have engaged with semiotic resources in all kinds of societies in history. In social semiotic theory, all modes of communication are given equally serious attention. Although history and ideology have assigned particular values to different modes, for example, the superiority of writing over speech in Western culture, social semiotic theory is concerned to show how all forms of meaning-making have as many similarities as differences (Gillen and Hall 2003).

The idea of meaning-making as choice was extended by Kress and van Leeuwen beyond language, into visual communication, with the publication of a visual grammar, *Reading Images: The Grammar of Visual Design* (1996 and 2nd edn 2006). As van Leeuwen (2000) points out, the analysis of words and images is not new. However, until the advent of a visual grammar (Kress and van Leeuwen 1996), such analyses were organised into discrete compartments in discrete disciplines: linguistics for language and art history for pictures. This made it difficult to compare, for example, a photograph and its caption, within the same underlying construction of reality. A social semiotic analysis is interested in comparing and contrasting different modes, analysing how they work together in multimodal ensembles. It attempts to look for common principles, semiotic functions and organising functions across different modes, drawing on Halliday's (1985) systemic functional grammar. In this grammar, the meanings of texts arise from the interplay between three types of meaning: ideational meaning (concerning who does what to whom, where and when); interpersonal meanings (which realise interactions and relationships between people), and textual meanings (which organise the text into a coherent message for the particular context of communication).

This perspective on communication as sign production, reception and transformation has been elaborated to include the resources of music/sound (van Leeuwen 1999), action (Martinec 2000; Kress *et al.* 2001), technology (Jewitt 2006) and their arrangement as multimodal ensembles (Kress and van Leeuwen 2001; van Leeuwen 2005).

### *Key concept: the social production of the sign*

The central concept in social semiotics is the sign, which is understood to be 'an instance of the use of a semiotic resource for purposes of communication' (van Leeuwen 2005: 285). In a sign, meaning (the signified) and form (the signifier) are brought together into a single unit. A basic assumption underlying social semiotics is the social production of the sign. Its focus is on how signs are socially produced and socially read. What signs stand for and how they are read is not static, pre-given or pre-determined, but affected by how people regulate semiotic resources in their social context of use. A social semiotic view of communication has its origin in critiques of Saussure's (1974) distinction between 'langue' and 'parole'. Saussure contrasts 'langue' as an abstraction, a closed system of normatively identical forms, with the unpredictable messiness of 'parole', which he defines as 'ephemeral', 'individual' and 'dependent on the will of the speaker'. This focus on 'langue' as a closed, stable system produces a unitary view of language and the idea of a homogenous community of speakers. Meaning-making is divorced from context and from material reality. Voloshinov (1973), in his critique of Saussure, theorises the utterance as 'a social phenomenon' and any semiotic analysis as rooted in a social and material base:

> 1 Ideology may not be divorced from the material reality of signs.
> 2 Signs may not be divorced from the concrete forms of social intercourse (seeing that the sign is part of organised social intercourse, and cannot exist, as such, outside it).
> 3 Communication and the forms of communication may not be divorced from the material basis.
>
> (Voloshinov 1973: 21)

The idea that signs are realised in material ways which move across semiotic systems has been critical to shifting our understanding of children's meaning-making as a complex multimodal, material practice, where children draw on and transform whatever modes and materials they deem appropriate, have 'to hand' or consider criterial at the time (Kress 1997a; Ormerod and Ivanic 2002; Lancaster 2001; Pahl 2003; Kenner 2004; UKLA/QCA 2004, 2005).

### *Key concept: motivated relationship between signifier and signified*

Social semiotics posits a motivated relationship between the signifier and the signified. According to Kress:

> Signs are the results of the interest of their makers, and this interest is expressed through the selection of apt signifiers for the expression of the sign maker's meaning.
>
> (Kress 1997a: 19)

A theory of a fully motivated relationship between the signifier and the signified contests the theory of arbitrariness in semiotics. This theory states that the relationship between signifier and signified is arbitrary, and that any form (signifier) can be used for any content. Following the Saussurian distinction between 'langue' and 'parole', an arbitrary semiotics is primarily concerned with 'langue' and the ideal speaker-hearer in a closed system of meaning-making which detaches the human being as agent and sign maker from the semiotic system. In contrast, a theory of the motivated sign situates itself firmly within the world of 'parole', the world of real users of signs, and the multiple and complex interventions between the users of signs, their meanings, practices and circumstances in which they are used. According to van Leeuwen, in social semiotics, the term 'langue' is replaced by 'semiotic resource', which he defines as 'actions, materials and artefacts we use for communicative purposes, whether produced physiologically or technologically, together with the ways in which these resources can be organised' (2005: 285).

In his article, 'Against arbitrariness: the social production of the sign as a foundational issue in critical discourse analysis,' Kress (1993) argues that the theory of the motivated relation of signifier and signified is 'an essential foundation and legitimation of the enterprise of critical reading' (1993: 169). The aim of critical reading, in critical discourse analysis and critical language awareness, is to make transparent the relations between language and power, which are operating through textual products (Fairclough 1989; Janks 2000). These relations include attention to the structures, locations and effects of power. Kress (1993) calls for attention not only to theorising how texts are socially produced within diverse contexts of power but also to how readers read such texts within relations of power, in order to produce a theory of the reading of texts.

### *Key concept: interested action*

A theory of the motivated sign comprises two aspects: the sign-maker is engaged in acts of sign-making which express his or her 'interested action' and the sign is being produced within certain constraints and possibilities. The term 'interested' refers to the fact that signs are never neutral but infused with the sign-maker's interests – the tension between what the sign-maker 'wanted to say' or 'needed to say' and what 'it was possible to say' at that moment.

Individual sign-makers do not act in isolation. The individual is a social agent with specific interests who is acting as a member of various groups with group interests: thus the individual's interests cannot be divorced from the histories of the social groups of which he or she is part. Individual interests may be divergent, resistant or convergent with group interests. The history of semiosis can be explained by reference to the histories of social groups within which actions of individual members have reshaped the available semiotic resources and continue to do so.

The term 'action' in 'interested action' points to the central role of human agency in meaning-making. Making meaning is action: a young child making marks on the page is an act of agency in which she inscribes herself on the world. Placing the human being in, and with, the social group at the centre of sign-making activity allows for the possibility of changes and shifts which are initiated by human processes and not by structures or systems. Acts of choice are determined by the sign-maker's interests, capacities for creativity and invention, and the constraints and possibilities offered by the formative role of structures in the context in which the meaning-making occurs. Acts of choice, however, can be highly constrained by the political and institutional structures in which they are embedded. This is starkly the case in relation to the digital divide, for example in Africa, where wide inequalities exist in relation to children's differential access to digital technologies and the Internet.

Every sign produced is a representation of the sign-maker's 'interest' and this interest always works at the micro levels of the individual sign-maker within the local context, and at broader, macro levels.

### *Key concept: design*

The notion of design is fundamental. We are *designers* of meaning (New London Group 1996; Cope and Kalantzis 2000; Kress 2000b): sign-makers as designers choose apt designs from available designs, according to his or her interests. The idea of 'competence in use' of a stable system of representation is contrasted with the idea of 'interested design' which starts with the interests and intentions of the designer, choosing and shaping available semiotic resources in relation to specific audiences and contexts. Designs are continuously shaped within history and culture and its available technologies for representation, as well as by an individual's relationship to identity and history. How people represent their meanings may be limited by the semiotic resources available, what Kress (1997a) calls 'what is to hand' and by students' competence in design. In this sense, design has futurity, rather than pastness, built into it:

> Focusing (through historical analysis) on how semiotic resources come to be as they are, multimodality can ask why they are as they are. This is powerful, enabling people to see how a reality comes to be represented and offering the potential to *imagine* it differently and to *redesign* it.
> (Jewitt 2008: 4)

### *Key concept: transformative action*

Central to social semiotic theory is the idea of change or 'transformative action'. In contrast to traditional views of language and literacy as a set of formal rules within a closed system, a transformative theory of meaning-making constructs meaning as a dynamic process of redesigning signs in response to other signs. This view implies that signs do not have fixed or intrinsic relationships but acquire meaning relationally within 'webs of signification' (Pahl and Rowsell 2006: 8) and are constantly in the process of being transformed. Meaning-making as a process of transformative action or 'work' produces change both in the object being transformed, as well as in the individual who is the agent of the transformation. Iedema (2003) uses the term 'resemiotization' to describe how 'meaning-making shifts from context to context, from practice to practice, or from one stage of a practice to the next' (2003: 41). In this process, meaning-making accrues different material realisations, becomes 'rematerialised' and in doing so, the meanings attached to the object or entity fundamentally shift. Resemiotisation is crucially interested in how materiality as 'expression' serves to realise 'the social, cultural and historical structures, investments and circumstances of our time' (2003: 50).

The idea of choice and transformation challenges the idea of the 're-usable sign', as Kress (1997b) refers to it. The 're-usable sign' underpins the notion of the stable sign that assumes that, in the making of meaning, we select signs from an existing system of signs to make up our particular sign. In this view, genres are stable text types that simply get reproduced again and again in the same way, with slight variations of form. The problem with this theory of use from an existing system is that it cannot account for change. In Kress's (1993) view, shifts in language use, genres and multimodal forms of communication can be explained by theorising social process at the heart of shifts in semiotic systems:

> The notion of sign that I am putting forward makes it possible to connect the specificity of semiotic forms, in any medium, with the specificities of social organisations and social histories, via the actions of social individuals in the production of signs . . . The history of any semiotic system, for instance the history of a language, is thus accounted for by the histories of social groups through the actions of their members in constantly making and remaking the semiotic system.
>
> (Kress 1993: 177)

This view allows for the move from the micro-level of an individual's reshaping of semiotic resources as part of, and linked into, larger macro-histories of semiotic systems.

## *Multimodality: key concepts*

Human communication is always produced from more than one mode. Modes never occur alone: they always form part of multimodal ensembles.

All texts are multimodal. Thus multimodality is a defining characteristic of communication and representation. Kress and van Leeuwen's interest in multimodality arose out of the inadequacy of current theories of language to account for the increasing complexity of contemporary electronic and digital communication systems, which combine sound, image, language and film through television, the computer, the Internet and mobile phones. In these multimodal forms of communication, language is decentred as well as the traditional boundaries between language, image, page layout and document design (Iedema 2003: 33). Multimodal social semiotics is interested in developing a theory and a methodology in which all modes are described together and describable together. This means understanding what modes can do, their different affordances, and how they work together in multimodal ensembles.

A mode is defined by Kress (2000a: 185) as a fully semiotically articulated means of representation and communication. In *Multimodal Discourse* (Kress and van Leeuwen 2001: 21–2), modes are defined as semiotic resources which allow the simultaneous realisation of discourses and types of action and interaction.

> Multimodality is concerned with signs and starts from the position that like speech and writing all modes consist of sets of semiotic resources – resources that people draw on and configure in specific moments and places to represent events and relations.
>
> (Jewitt 2008: 1)

Modes can be realised in multiple media: for example, narrative can be thought of a mode because it has the capacity for multiple forms of articulation across media. Colour is also an example of a mode because it too can be articulated across media (Kress and van Leeuwen 2002). Modes are disseminated through technologies or media: for example, the history of print involves the shift from the use of the hand in the Middle Ages for writing manuscripts, to the use of the printing press in the sixteenth century, to the use of electronic and digital technologies in the twenty-first century. Each technology has produced a material change in texts, our relationship to them, and how we make use of them.

Modes have grammars and communicative effects. Take, for example, the mode of gesture: each gesture communicates a meaning but the repertoire of gestures that an individual person uses is culturally specific, and shifts according to social occasions or contexts of use. For example, eye contact may be thought of as a basic physiological action. But there are multiple ways of making eye contact, with different meanings attached to each one. In South Africa, the use of eye contact has cultural variations, depending on who is talking to whom and the power and gender relations which are operating. Men and women use eye contact differently, for example, in contexts of courting. For some South Africans, not making eye contact shows respect for elders. For other South Africans, making eye contact shows respect for elders and not making eye contact shows disrespect. Thus, how people use eye contact changes according to contexts of culture and use.

A mode has materiality. This refers to the ways in which the mode is made into material or substantialised. Kress refers to 'the stuff' (1997a) that a culture uses as the means for expression of its meanings. Materiality can be physical in the forms of sounds, marks, textures, shapes and forms. In this sense, it can be seen or perceived, felt, heard, tasted or touched. At this level it can be seen as the 'interface' between the natural and cultural world. However, materiality can work at different levels, depending on the degrees of transformation the mode has gone through in cultural production in specific contexts and the degrees of sophistication in this work. Think, for example, of the degrees of sophistication of modal transformation in the production of video and computer games. Materiality can also have a non-physical appearance in language in the range of words that are spoken, or in sound, where sounds have been finely worked on to produce a particular sound.

The materiality of semiotic modes is related to the sensory possibilities of the body. Thus, the possibilities that 'sight' or 'touch' offer push the boundaries of 'seeing' and 'touching' in terms of 'what can be seen' and 'what can be touched'. For example, the temporality of the human voice ensures that particular speech sounds are organised into a sequence. This sequence can then be used for different semiotic purposes and for different effects. The concept of multimodality is inseparable from bodies. Bodies produce multimodality through how they are constituted sensually and how these senses act on the world and are acted on. The senses are highly sophisticated in the information they provide us with: they do not act in isolation in most cases and this fact 'guarantees' the multimodality of our semiotic world (Kress 2000a: 184). This is the biological aspect of multimodality. The brain's ability to move across modes and senses is called synaesthetic activity. This process of transduction takes place constantly and is not always visible, as our brains 'translate' one sense into another, for example, representing a feeling in words, a touch in sound, a smell in colours. Some people have certain senses more finely developed than do others, and this is present in their representational activity.

Modes, as culturally shaped semiotic resources, have semiotic potential. They have affordances and constraints: this implies that they can produce certain communicative effects and not others. The term 'affordances' comes from Gibson (1979) who defines affordances as the potential uses of a given object, stemming from the perceivable properties of the object. van Leeuwen elaborates:

> Because perception is selective, depending on the needs and interests of the perceivers, different perceivers will notice different affordances. But

> those that remain unnoticed continue to exist objectively, latent in the object, waiting to be discovered.
>
> (van Leeuwen 2005: 273)

On the distinction between the different affordances of writing and image as a move from narrative to display, Kress has written that the two modes produce quite distinctly different takes on the world, different images of that world, and different dispositions by their users – whether as text-producers or as text-consumers – towards the world:

> Narrative and display each have the most fundamental consequences for an individual's or a culture's orientation in the world, so this shift is bound to have equally fundamental repercussions in social, cultural, political and economic practices, and in the subjectivities of individuals.
>
> (Kress 1997b: 16–17)

In education, there is increasing interest in the study of multimodal communication and representation, and its implications for multimodal pedagogies (Stein 2007). In a special edition of *Linguistics and Education* edited by Lemke (2000), researchers examine multimodality in subjects across the curriculum, particularly mathematics and science. O'Halloran (2000, 2004) uses a systemic-functional perspective to dissect the multiple sign systems operating in the mathematics classroom, which make the pedagogical discourse very dense. This contributes to the inherent difficulties in the teaching and learning of mathematics. Baker and Street (2006) investigate multimodal numeracies as a social practice and have identified different modes of representation in mathematics education, including actional, diagrammatic and symbolic modes. They suggest, like O'Halloran, that problems of switching between such modes may be a source of students' difficulties in the subject.

Lemke (2000) focuses on the science classroom. Investigating students in their final year of secondary school, Lemke found that students were expected to meet stringent demands for mastery of multiple, hybrid multi-media genres and their associated genre-specific literacies at an advanced level. The key point Lemke makes is that it is not enough to gain mastery of one modality: scientific concepts, as in mathematics, are articulated *across* these modes and media:

> it is only in the integration of these various aspects that the whole concept exists . . . So we do not have so much an exact translatability among verbal statements, mathematical formulas, and visual-graphical or material-operational representations as a complex set of co-ordinating practices for functionally integrating our uses of them. And these co-ordinating practices must be learned in each case as a difficult and specialized form of multi-literacy.
>
> (Lemke 2000: 246)

Kress *et al.*'s (2001) study on multimodal teaching and learning in the science classroom provides a set of conceptual tools for analysing multimodality in pedagogical settings. It presents a detailed account of how teachers use action, gesture, modelling, speech, writing, image and role play to communicate scientific knowledge, and the importance of materiality as a semiotic resource. Kress *et al.* make clear the integral connection between formal issues of representation, such as genres and modes, and the shaping of knowledge: certain modes are used to convey particular content in ways which other modes cannot. For example, the genre of 'a conceptual map' to represent the circulation of the blood represents the entity 'blood circulation' in a way which is different to the genre of 'a story of the journey of the blood'. This study opens up important questions around which mode to use to best represent particular content: is the structure of an electronic circuit best represented in writing or in image? It also explores what it means to 'talk' or 'write' like a scientist, in other words, how learners take on the discourses or social languages (Gee 1996) of science in ways which make sense.

There is a growing body of work exploring multimodality in English education (e.g. Goodwyn 2005; Stein and Newfield 2006). *English in Urban Classrooms* (Kress *et al.* 2005) provides a multimodal perspective of contemporary school English in three state co-educational, ethnically diverse secondary schools in inner London. This study asks: How is English made? What is it like? Whereas previous studies of the English classroom have focused on the role of 'talk' and on language in its written and spoken form as the main mode of communication, this research pays attention to all the culturally shaped resources through which the subject is realised, including image, gesture, layout, writing and speech. The varied visual displays and spatial arrangements of classrooms can be understood as multimodal signs that inflect a particular relationship to history and culture around what constitutes the subject English. The importance of this study is not only in its findings but in its methodological framework: it presents a multimodal perspective as a new methodology or 'way of looking' at subject English, 'so that we might actually get a full understanding of its reality, in all ways, in the experience of students and teachers alike, in any one classroom' (Kress *et al.* 2005: 1). Bhattacharya *et al.* (2007) build on and extend this research on school English in order to explore its relevance to English in post-colonial sites in a time of globalisation. Developing the idea of the textual cycle, that is, the selection of texts and the pedagogic processes and practices within which texts are embedded and through which they are realised by individual teachers, they investigate the policy-practice nexus in English classrooms in Delhi, Johannesburg and London. This multimodal and international perspective shows how the policies mediated by agencies of the state, the school, the English department and individual teachers are inflected and refracted through the textual cycle to position teachers in particular ways. This study also demonstrates that the textual cycle as a unit of analysis has rich potential as a manageable and highly significatory sign.

In a post-colonial study of 'indigenous multimodality' in Brazil, Menezes de Souza (2005) shows the power of the multimodal literacy practices of the Kashinawa people who inhabit the Amazonian state of Acre in northwestern Brazil. This literacy, which combines non-alphabetic forms of writing, including images, colour, symbols, words and spatial design in complex forms of meaning-making, can be seen as alternate to the dominant literacy of schooling, which is grapho-centric. Menezes de Souza uses this example of 'local' writing practice in indigenous communities to critique the deficit and stereotypical model of indigenous people constructed in indigenous schools in Brazil through the teaching and learning materials and literacy pedagogies. Other examples of 'indigenous multimodality' are described in Kendrick *et al.*'s (2006) work in Uganda; Newfield and Stein (2000), Janks (2006), Newfield and Maungedzo (2006) and Archer's (2006) research in South Africa; and Smagorinsky *et al.*'s (2005) case study of a Native-American student's mask-making practices in a US high school.

## New Literacy Studies

New Literacy Studies refers to an influential, growing body of work, socio-cultural in orientation, in which literacy is viewed as a social practice embedded in relations of power, history and culture. New Literacy Studies is an interdisciplinary field, drawing on related research in cultural anthropology, applied linguistics, cultural psychology and situated cognition theory. Researchers have used these insights in making visible 'invisible' local literacies, including Scribner and Cole (1981), Heath (1983), Street (1984; 1993; 2001), Barton (1994), Baynham (1995), Gee (1996), Barton and Hamilton (1998) Barton *et al.* (2000). In South Africa the New Literacy Studies orientation is evident in Prinsloo and Breier's (1996) research into adult literacy in the Social Uses of Literacy Project (SOUL), the Children's Early Literacy Learning (CELL) research (Bloch *et al.* 2001; Prinsloo 2004; Prinsloo and Stein 2005; Stein and Slonimsky 2006) and the work investigating academic literacy, higher education and social justice of the Language Development Group at the University of Cape Town (Thesen and van Pletzen 2006).

Scholars working in this area challenge firmly held, traditional views of literacy in which literacy is narrowly defined simply as the ability 'to read and write'. In this view, literacy is conceptualised as an autonomous, static, neutral set of cognitive skills that can be taught and learnt using the same 'universal' model in any context in the world. This definition powerfully frames how those involved with literacy – curriculum planners, schools, teachers, children, parents and communities – work with literacy. In contrast, New Literacy Studies constructs literacy as a resource, a set of social practices which are domain specific, varied and multiple, tied to specific uses and functions within social institutions of power and access which shape it in diverse ways. A key contribution of New Literacy Studies has been to provide evidence of how literacy varies across cultural time and space. Using concepts such as 'literacy events' and 'literacy practices' to describe the different occasions, contexts and concepts which constitute people's relations to and engagements with literacy, research in the New Literacy Studies, often ethnographic in style, provides 'thick descriptions' (Geertz 1983) of the complex, changing uses of multiple literacies embedded in particular domains or settings.

Working within a social justice agenda, researchers within this field are interested in investigating the relationship between 'schooled literacy' as a particular form of cultural capital, and other forms of literacy which children and adults use in their everyday lives outside of school. Such investigations help to throw light on how learners navigate the relationship between the forms of knowledge produced in school and the 'ways of knowing' sustained and cultivated in domains outside of school, such as the home (Baker *et al.* 1996). These forms of knowledge are differently valued and privileged within these different sites, a fact that has important consequences for students' learning, motivation, identities, and successful integration into the school environment. Practices around what counts as 'literacy' in these different domains is a political and ideological issue. In what Bartlett and Holland call 'a paradigmatic revolution' (2002: 11), literacy is reconceptualised as a 'practice-based account' through Street's (1984) concept of the ideological model which positions literacy as a multilayered 'field' in which issues of value and access to resources, culture and power are intimately tied up in how it is enacted and constituted in material settings.

Barton and Hamilton (1998) have summed up a social theory of literacy using a set of six propositions:

1 Literacy is best understood as a set of social practices; these can be inferred from events that are mediated by written texts.
2 There are different literacies associated with different domains of life.
3 Social institutions and power relationships pattern literacy practices, and some literacies become more dominant, visible and influential than others.
4 Literacy practices are purposeful and embedded in broader social goals and cultural practices.
5 Literacy is historically situated.
6 Literacy practices change, and new ones are frequently acquired through processes of informal learning and sense making.

(Barton and Hamilton 1998: 7)

## Literacy events and literacy practices

The concepts of 'literacy events' and 'literacy practices' are central to the language of description developed in New Literacy Studies for viewing literacy as a social practice. The term 'literacy events' is derived from Heath's (1983) *Ways with Words*, a seminal ethnographic study of children's language and literacy acquisition in the Roadville, Trackton and townspeople communities in the Piedmont Carolinas. Literacy events are those occasions in which 'the talk revolves around a piece of writing'. Literacy events have social interactional rules that 'regulate the type and amount of talk about what is written and define ways in which oral language reinforces, denies, extends, or sets aside the written material' (Heath 1983: 386). Barton and Hamilton (1998: 7) refer to literacy events as activities in social contexts where literacy has a role; they are 'observable episodes which arise from practices and are in turn shaped by practices'.

The concept of 'practice' is used in a range of ways by different researchers. Street (1995, 2000) uses the term 'literacy practices' to describe the specificity of literacies in particular places and times. His concept of 'literacy practices' works at a higher level of abstraction than 'literacy events' and 'refers to both behaviour and the social and cultural conceptualisations that give meaning to the uses of reading and/or writing'. Literacy events are classified as 'empirical' instances in which literacy plays a crucial part. Literacy practices, however, consist of 'folk models of those events and the ideological preconceptions which underpin them' (Street 1995: 2).

The multiple perspectives of 'practice' used in socio-cultural approaches to literacy and numeracy research are explored by Baynham and Baker (2002) who point out that a characteristic of practices is both their 'situatedness' in particular contexts or environments and their role in producing, reproducing as well as challenging contexts and environments. They emphasise that 'context is produced through practices' rather than situations or contexts providing 'a static backdrop' against which practices are played out.

The focus on local literacy practices, a great strength of New Literacy Studies, has been challenged by Brandt and Clinton in their article 'The Limits of the Local' (2002) in which they argue that it is impossible now to think about local literacies without situating them within the context of globalisation. In other words, the local and the global are inextricably tied up together. They also assert that social practice theory is too 'human-centred' and does not take into account the role that non-human actors – like technologies – play in meaning-making. The advantage of the concept of multimodality, they argue, is 'the language it provides for talking about technologies as actants at the scenes of reading and writing, as active and ideological social agents towards which readers and writers orient' (Brandt and Clinton 2006: 254).

## Situated meanings: social languages, activities and identities

Researchers in New Literacy Studies operate with socio-cultural theories around mind, learning and society which assume that the human mind is 'embodied, situated and social' (Cope and Kalantzis 2000: 30). Drawing on work in cognitive science, social cognition and socio-cultural orientations to language and literacy (Wertsch 1985; Cazden 1988; Lave and Wenger 1991; Gee 1992, 2003; Wenger 1998; Rogoff 2003) these theories share the view that how human beings make meaning is linked to their experiences of how deeply knowledge is contextualised in specific domains and practices, which in themselves are socially and historically situated. These experiences are not stored in the mind/brain in forms of language but in 'dynamic images' tied to perception both of the world and of our own bodies, internal states and feelings (Gee 2004). Meaning-making is 'sense making'. It is tied to what human beings understand they can actually do with an object, event or procedure, and to the extent that such doing makes sense within this person's frames of reference. Making sense of and learning a new practice or activity involves being part of or entering a community of practice (Lave and Wenger 1991), a group of learners engaged in a common practice centred on a specific domain of knowledge. As Gee (2004) points out, situated meanings are rooted in embodied experience. The ability to see patterns and apply patterns flexibly to new contexts of meaning is at the basis of the development of mastery of a practice.

Language use is a form of embodied engagement with the world. Gee (1996) claims that language learning and the acquisition of 'social languages' are intimately tied to questions of identity and the social practices in which those identities are embedded. 'Social languages' are the particular kinds or styles of language that we need in order to accomplish specific goals within specific contexts of meaning. School requires students to develop discourse specific, academic social languages, which in turn become associated with specific identities associated with the practices around that particular discipline. Acquiring academic social languages involves having access to models, networks and practices of those who have gained more mastery of the language in the midst of practice. Gee's (2003) work on video games describes them as complex multimodal environments, in which players come to learn about and appreciate interrelations within and across multiple sign systems (images, words, actions, symbols, artifacts). Video games work with some of the best learning principles:

> They situate meaning in a multimodal space through embodied experiences to solve problems and reflect on the intricacies of the designs of imagined worlds and the design of both real and imagined social relationships and identities in the modern world.
>
> (Gee 2003: 48)

## Home, community and school

New Literacy Studies has provided valuable insights into how social languages and literacies in specific domains are produced, legitimated and valued. The relevant domains of interest for the purposes of this research are home and school. If one assumes that literacy is inseparable from broader socio-cultural, political and economic issues relating to how societies constitute themselves, then issues of power and access are central to discussions around literacy and development, literacy and schooling. Who gets access to literacy resources, how, and in which languages, is a critical issue in post-apartheid education in South Africa, where issues of redress, poverty and equity form part of the national debate around transformation. These are part of much larger debates around new capitalism, globalisation and increasing gaps between the rich, who have access to multiple resources and cultural capital, and the poor, who do not have the same access or networks. Gaining access to dominant literacies and languages is an ongoing struggle for the majority of children in South Africa, who speak home languages which are not privileged in mainstream schooling, and who have access to ways of knowing which are different from those privileged in schools. This leaves children with little option but to abandon their identities rooted in 'out of school' knowledge and cultural resources and take on the socially situated identities of schooling and related academic social languages. The problem in South Africa, however, is that schools and teachers, on the whole, do not have the technological or academic resources needed to provide contextually rich, engaging learning environments for the majority of children. Disaffection, hostility, distress and drop-out rates are the result, with the concomitant social and political consequences (Christie 1992; Taylor and Vinjevold 1999).

New Literacy Studies has produced research which demonstrates the nuances of local literacies and ways of knowing in different domains of knowledge. Such research can be used productively to challenge models of deficit with models of difference, showing that norms and standards are cultural constructions, not 'givens', and that the future of literacy lies in recognising the multiplicity of identities, languages and literacies which constitute the world. As Luke (2005) has pointed out, teachers now have to deal with versions of 'epistemological diversity' in which students bring to class 'complex, multiple and blended background knowledges, identities and discourses, constructing identity and practice from a range of scripts that go far beyond the "two worlds" metaphors of multicultural education' (2005: xiii).

## Southern African cultural studies and the local

A central aim of this research is to study children's multimodal meaning-making as culturally and historically embedded within local communicative practices. The context from which we speak shapes the knowledge we produce

(Canagarajah 2005: 14). In every sense, this study is itself a complex sign, inflected with my own subject position, interests and perspectives on what I understand to be 'the local'. Regional/local studies in African and Southern African culture and literature have been essential reading in developing an understanding of the histories of representational forms and genres that have influenced the children's production of multi-semiotic texts. Southern African cultural studies is broad-ranging in its research methodologies, foci of enquiry and epistemological standpoints. However, a large body of work which draws on anthropology, history, literary studies and sociology is concerned with the study of aesthetics and popular culture in Africa, its processes and practices.

The research I have drawn on has been mainly in the areas of oral literature, particularly storytelling and performance genres. Key scholars in this area include Scheub (1975), Bauman (1986), Finnegan (1992), Hofmeyr (1994, 2004), Coplan (1994), Furniss and Gunner (1995), Barber (1997), James (1999) and Gunner (2004, 2006). In the area of the visual arts, I have drawn on the work of Dell (1998), Nettleton *et al.* (2003, 2004) and Nel and Leibhammer (1998) in relation to fertility/child figures in the Southern African region. In the section that follows, I discuss some key concepts that underpin these studies and that are pertinent to this study.

## Oral performance as socio-cultural practice

Until recently, much of the scholarship on African oral literature has focused on oral texts as examples of folkloric artefacts, as disembodied, ahistorical, linguistic and literary objects. Discussion of these traditions has concentrated on the formal analyses of genres, content and the linguistic and literary features of the oral texts. Finnegan (1992), in her guide to anthropological research practices in oral traditions and the verbal arts, has noted a recent shift in interest to detailed study of oral *practices* on the ground, in specific local sites and contexts. These studies focus on the communicative and discursive contexts in which the text is being produced and include attention to the socio-cultural and historical contexts in which the meaning-making is being negotiated. This includes foregrounding the role of human individual agency, voices, emotions and creativity, the power relations between and among participants and the broader socio-cultural, political and institutional contexts in which the text is being produced:

> One theme is greater concern with individual voices, repertoire and creativity, part of the move within anthropology and other disciplines from 'structure' to 'agency'. Another is an emerging interest in work on the emotions and in aesthetic and expressive facets of human activity. A more explicit focus on 'meaning' comes in too, both meanings to be gleaned from the 'text' and those expressed through a multiplicity of

> voices. What is involved, further, is more than just the voice of the composer/poet (in the past pictured as *the* central figure), but also the other participants who help to form the work and mediate its meaning and the dynamics through which this occurs.
>
> (Finnegan 1992: 51)

Bauman (1986) in his work on oral storytelling, positions himself in the tradition of Bakhtin (1981) and others who have maintained an integrated vision of the social and the poetic in the study of oral literature. The structure of the event is a systemic interplay of numerous social, contextual and textual factors, including the relations between the narrated events (the events recounted in the narrative) and the narrative event itself (the actual performance event itself). Furniss and Gunner (1995) in their volume on power, marginality and African literature, trace the boundary shifts that have been occurring in the concept of 'performance' as social activity. These include a constitutive notion of textuality, placing the authorial voice in intertextual relation to other voices both internally and externally. The 'traditional' and the 'modern' are not positioned as separate categories but as current labels under internal cultural debate. The 'oral' and the 'written' are viewed as part of communicative practices, thus directing our attention to the particular communicative processes of 'being oral'/orality rather than objects that are specimens or 'oral literature' (Furniss and Gunner 1995: 2–3). Barber (1997) has noted the degree to which political and social struggle is a key factor in African oral literature: popular oral performance is always shaped by political pressures and made up of cultural resources which are dynamic and always shifting.

## 'Tradition' and 'modernity'

The term 'tradition' has multiple meanings: it can refer to 'established ways of doing things', heritage, culture, customs, habits, collective ways of doing things, or passing down ideas, artefacts and practices from one generation to another. It is associated with things being 'old' or having arisen in some organic way, as a result of natural processes, rather than imposed or constructed ones (Finnegan 1992: 7). The term 'modernity' according to Giddons (1991), refers to the institutions and modes of behaviour established in post-feudal Europe but which have become world-historical in their impact on the twentieth (and twenty-first) centuries. He equates 'modernity' with industrialism, global capitalism, surveillance, the nation-state and the rise of organisation – the regularised control of social relations across indefinite time-space distances.

Theorising the relationship of 'the past' or 'tradition' in relation to 'modernity' and contemporary cultural forms is central to the field of Southern African cultural studies. Tradition and modernity are not in a binary, essentialised relation but multiple, interpenetrative and part of ongoing semiosis. The act of interpreting textual products and practices involves understanding the contexts in which they are created, interpreted and distributed. Such interpretations cannot be divorced from the histories of these genres. This assumes that texts and communicative practices are not autonomous and discrete but form part of the making of consciousness and its expressions within social formations of power and culture. Such texts and practices form part of the active process in which human beings, as cultural actors, use historically salient cultural categories to construct their self-awareness. According to Comaroff and Comaroff:

> The poetry of representation, in short, is not an aesthetic embellishment of a 'truth' that lies elsewhere. [It is] the stuff of everyday thought and action – of the human consciousness through which culture and history construct each other.
>
> (Comaroff and Comaroff 1987: 207)

In a discussion on the continuing use of 'tradition' as a conceptual category, Coplan (1994) invokes the work of Hobsbawm and Ranger (1984) which demonstrates that tradition, far from being something organic, immutable and unchanging, was deliberately 'invented' in the service of fostering power in relation to political and national identities. He adds:

> The notion of immemorial traditions of performance, so popular with participants and folklorists alike, all too often evaporates under the scrutiny of historical research.
>
> (Coplan 1994: 17)

Coplan's analysis of the word music of South Africa's Basotho migrants suggests that the performance of these aural genres does draw on 'organic traditions of both discursive and practical consciousness' and that there is value to rethinking the concept of tradition, 'not simply as the reified emblems of authority but the immanence of the past in the cultural certainties of the present'. Such 'immanence' is what persists 'by virtue of both deliberate and undeliberate handing down, the metaphors of others with which our mouths are full' (Coplan 1994: 19).

In a study of *isicathamiya,* a contemporary, urban form of music and performance from KwaZulu-Natal, Gunner (2004; 2006) describes the extent to which this genre of popular culture is hybrid, drawing on older cultural genres such as the wedding dances of *idwendwe*, at the same time mixing them with transatlantic appropriations from acapella barbershop music and Welsh male choral music. She argues that this genre is dialogic with social life, having the capacity to negotiate 'the present painful dilemmas about belonging' at both micro and macro levels. In a study of performance and identity in the *kiba* songs of women migrants in South Africa, James (1999) explores the relationship between *kiba* as a 'traditional' music in South Africa, and the various ways in which migrant women have reappropriated the genre, formerly a male preserve, for their own contemporary, communicative purposes. This study foregrounds the importance of the material and socio-political constituencies of the women and their audiences. James demonstrates the extent to which the music and songs produced are not 'merely passive reflectors of already constituted social relationships and identities, but play a role in formulating and cementing these'. The migrant women are not passive 'victims' of capitalist economic processes in relation to the state, but are 'actors, drawing on both personal and cultural resources to shape their choices and structure their lives' (James 1999: 187). In a discussion on the relationship between 'tradition' and 'modernity' she argues that their assertion of 'home' through the use of this genre of performance 'of origin' should be understood 'not as a sign of nostalgia' but as a project of social advancement. In this way, cultural resources 'of origin' are continuously invoked to serve the personal, collective and identity interests of the makers within the moment of making.

The analyses of oral performance genres focus predominantly on language as the dominant mode of communication in performance. Although these studies pay attention to other modes such as sound, gesture and action, they are not accorded the same value as language, and hence often under-analysed. It seems that this study of children's meaning-making can contribute to the field of Southern African cultural studies through its recognition that oral performances are multimodal, multi-semiotic, communicational ensembles in which language is only one mode in which meaning is being made. Studies of local oral performances, such as *isicathamiya*, are wonderful examples of multimodal performance, in which meaning is being made in a multiplicity of modes and media, in every layer, and in different places within each layer in the communicational ensemble. Analyses of such performances, which take account of these multi-layerings, could reveal the complexity of this cultural form as a social semiotic practice.

Finnegan's more recent work, *Communicating: the Multiple Modes of Human Interconnection* (2002), presents a 'fresh view of human communication' which emphasises the varied modes through which humans communicate and the multi-sensory resources we draw on to interconnect with others. In a critique of dominant models which view communication as a mental, cognitive activity, Finnegan challenges these models for 'stopping at the neck' (Farnell 1995: 9) by equating communication with verbal language only (in its spoken and written forms) and for therefore representing a 'narrow view on communication, and with it, on human life'. This logocentrism has become associated with grand narratives of modernisation, Western forms of post-enlightenment rationality, objectivity and scientific thinking, alphabetic forms and writing, and has 'left behind' the more 'primitive' ritual, tradition, emotion and magic

(Finnegan 2002: 27). Finnegan refers to the legacy of scholars such as Austin (1962), Birdwhistell (1970), Bakhtin (1981, 1986), Bauman (1986) and Hymes (1996) who have shown how communication is communicatively constituted, produced and reproduced by communicative acts. In this view, society is constituted not as a predetermined entity over and above individuals, but emergent in and through their actions, emotions and experiences, within social worlds which they are part of and which they constitute. This paradigm shift from a view of human communication as autonomous, static and passive, to one in which human beings are active interconnecting agents, purposeful meaning-makers, who make and remake their meanings within and in response to their affective and social worlds, refocuses our attention on the communicative potential inherent in human beings:

> Communicating is envisaged as creative human process . . . it encompasses the many modes of human interacting and living, both near and distant – through smells, sounds, touches, sights, movements, embodied engagements and materials objects. These interconnecting processes are necessary ones for collective human life.
>
> (Finnegan 2002: 5)

A rich example of multimodality at work in Africa is present in contemporary Congolese music, which Mbembe (2006) describes as 'at once poetry, dance and prayer', locating its aesthetic signification in a world of sensations. He describes the 'totality of sensations, pleasures and energies provoked by a particular work, or set in motion in the subject listening or dancing to it.' Congolese music gives a central role to orality and voice, all of which takes place within the context of plural languages and reciprocal interpenetration between different artistic genres and improvisational practices:

> All of these properties give Congolese music a distinctive quality. These works have developed an aesthetic made up of fantasies and productive counterpoints as well as discords and distortions. . . . This interweaving of forms, genres and contents make it possible to invent original compositions where words, the world of images, appearances and sounds merge together, producing flurries of occasional brilliance and primitive melodies which evoke tears and suffering as much as they do ecstacy . . . This is a music where the emotions are always in conflict, where the theatrical and the oneiric are superimposed on one another across savage oceans of sounds, screams and noise. Figures and gestures drawn from popular theatre, with its farcical and comical aspects, its exaggerated disguises and its untidy and brightly coloured costumes, are brought to bear on any musical.
>
> (Mbembe 2006: 75)

From a social semiotic perspective, meaning-making is always a process of transformation, in which cultural groupings use and transform the semiotic resources of communication available to them to express their interests, within different kinds of communicative practices. What people make can be viewed as 'points of fixing' within semiosis. These points of fixing contain the past, the present, the future. They are part of the chains of meaning-making, and in constant transformation as culture draws new materials into communicative processes.

## Childhood, democracy and children's rights in South Africa

This exploration of children's representations of their inner and outer worlds cannot take place in isolation from dominant constructs of childhood in South Africa, and issues of social justice in relation to children's rights. How children are perceived, engaged with, represented, managed and positioned within different domains of power in everyday life provide evidence for these abiding social constructions. They also influence children's self-concepts within their social environments and how they choose to represent their lives, interests and experiences.

South Africa has an appalling record with regard to its children. The plight of South African black children and their profound suffering under apartheid rule is well known. Apartheid influenced all aspects of children's lives, which in the case of black children, were uniformly destructive and debilitating. These included the systematic destruction of family life through the migrant labour system, gross inequalities between black and white children in the distribution of resources and social services, legalised racism and institutionalised violence (Rock 1997). Children played significant roles in the liberation struggle in South Africa: the 1976 Soweto uprisings were led by high-school students who refused to be taught through the medium of Afrikaans. These children were victims of Bantu Education, a racially segregated, unequal system of education enforced during the apartheid years, in which African children were trained to fulfil the white minority's need for certain forms of labour. Curricula and pedagogies were implemented which constructed students as passive, rote learners, authority dependent, uncritical and obediently subservient to white rule (Kallaway 1984; Hartshorne 1992; Christie 1992).

According to the United Nations Convention on the Rights of the Child of 1989, the state is responsible for safeguarding children's physical and psychological well-being. However, in the case of black children, apartheid was blatantly neglectful and abusive (Straker and Moosa 1994). Describing the effects of apartheid on children's lives, Knutsson and O'Dea have stated:

> Apartheid was many things. Among the most revolting of its obscenities was the state-based and state-supported movement against children, whom common morals and international law expect the state to protect. It was a movement against children that culminated in a brutal offensive when they dared to claim the most elemental of rights such as the reasonable freedom of assembly or choice of language of instruction . . . Consequently, the state hit back with all its force: detaining, brutalising, starving and killing children who were seen as 'threats' to a state armoured in steel. Tens of thousands were directly affected and millions suffered indirectly . . . In the end all of them were repeatedly punished for asking for the simple right to a decent childhood and a hopeful future.
>
> (Knutsson and O'Dea 1998: 6)

The extent of children's suffering under apartheid has been well documented by scholars such as Burman and Reynolds (1986), Reynolds (1989), Jones (1993), Dawes and Donald (1994), Henderson (1999), Chubb and Van Dijk (2001). These studies focus on the need to study children not as immature, future adults, but *as children*, as visible, significant actors in families, communities, homes and schools, and as active participants in culture:

> We must also recognise that children are not just passive recipients of culture, not just half and three-quarter adults: children, as much as men and women, *have* culture, are *part* of culture, and are *makers* of culture.
>
> (Jones 1993: 6)

Jones has written of the need for scholars to gather testimonies from children about their lives and experiences in order to gain important details and insights into how children perceive their lived realities and how they navigate their way through arduous social situations of migrancy, fragmented family structures, living conditions of extreme poverty, violence and hardship, and disrupted schooling. Referring to 'the national neglect' of children in South Africa as 'nothing less than a systematic assault on childhood itself', he calls for a co-ordinated, ongoing and action-orientated programme of interdisciplinary research on childhood:

> If post-apartheid society is to make any significant difference to their [children's] lot, it is therefore critical that the particular realities of all this country's children be documented, understood and fully represented in the process of its definition. There remains much to be learnt about, and also from, South Africa's children.
>
> (Jones 1993: 204)

Henderson (1999) has noted how prevailing idealised notions of childhood can deny children the responsibilities they patently have in many social contexts as well as the agency they bring to bear in moulding society.

In post-apartheid South Africa, children under 18 years constitute almost half (44 per cent) of the population. The ANC government has committed itself to principles of redress and equality in improving the lives of its children. A Bill of Rights is the cornerstone of democracy in South Africa. The government's commitment to children is reflected in section 28 of the Bill of Rights in the Constitution, its ratification in 1995 of the United Nations Conventions of the Rights of the Child, and its establishment in 1996 of a National Plan of Action for South African children. However, it has been recognised that protecting children means addressing constitutionally the vast material inequalities which continue to plague South African children, substantially impeding their growth and development. Although the Children's Act 38 of 2005 takes forward the government's commitment to protecting the socio-economic rights and human rights of children, much work needs to be done on the ground in providing protection and care for South African children. The *South African Child Gauge 2006* (Morson *et al.* 2006) states that more than half of South Africa's children live in extreme poverty, in homes which are too poor to buy basic necessities and where the average household income is R800 or less. In these households, children do not get enough food, social conditions are unhealthy and education often absent or below standard. Sixty-four per cent of children living in poverty are black and 4 per cent are white. Leatt (2006: 19) has noted that South Africa has such high levels of child poverty because of the apartheid legacy, the high levels of unemployment in the country, and the fact that poor communities and households are the most heavily affected by the HIV/AIDS pandemic. Families living with this disease are likely to lose wage or self-employment income if an income-earner gets sick and this has the effect of deepening poverty.

In terms of education, the government has committed itself to transforming the education system through providing all children with access to compulsory basic schooling, where previously there was none. Through outcomes-based curriculum innovations such as Curriculum 2005 (Department of Education 1996) and the Revised National Curriculum documents (Department of Education 2002), the government is attempting to transform teaching and learning practices along more democratic, learner-centred lines. However, the gap between policies, implementation and delivery remains a large one and structural and distributional inequalities among South African children and their families continue to exist, affecting each child's life chances. Despite current redress, equity and rights initiatives to address the plight of South African children, a culture of violence persists, with ongoing, damaging consequences to South African children. There has been a decline in politically inspired violence, but criminal and domestic violence continues unabated (Seedat *et al.* 2001). Much of the focus of current local research is on developing intervention programmes in the contexts of childhood adversity (Rock 1997; Donald *et al.* 2000).

A major aim of this research is to draw attention to the texts and meaning-making practices of South African children whose voices are generally unrecognised, silenced or marginalised in mainstream classrooms. Through providing evidence of children's creativity, social and cultural awareness and resourcefulness in conditions of childhood adversity, it aims to raise the status of children in South Africa. The analyses of children's communicative practices point to their acute awareness of social and political issues within contexts of poverty, their sensitivity to pain and violence and the dangers of everyday life. At the same time, the texts they produce are full of humour and playfulness, often with ironic, witty comment on their social relationships and encounters of the everyday.

In this research, children are positioned as active transformers of culture. This orientation locates itself within scholarship which conceptualises children as active participants in domestic and community life, as human beings who have rights, resources, creativity, opinions, judgements and agency. There are numerous instances in this book of how children have taken agency in the assertion of their identities and have demonstrated in remarkable ways their rights to be acknowledged as resourceful makers of meaning across different languages and in different modes. The majority of the children in this study are poor, living in contexts of deprivation, harm and violence, in single female-headed households in urban townships and informal settlements. Some of the children are living in children-headed households with no adults. The ANC government has committed itself to rebuilding the education system in South Africa. However, rebuilding structures and curriculum processes needs to go hand in hand with transforming teaching and learning practices in classrooms. Giving children equitable opportunities to represent their worlds – their voices, cultures, histories, feelings and opinions – in the modes and languages they choose and feel comfortable with is an educational right: it is part and parcel of how children's right to basic education needs to be conceptualised.

Children's meaning-making practices are cultural processes which form part of the production of culture in a society. An important aim of this research is to argue that children's production of culture is a capacity worth strengthening in building a democratic culture. In arguing this position, Appadurai's (2002) work on culture as 'a capacity worth building' in contexts of development and poverty, is very useful. In seeking a new approach to answering the question on why culture matters for development and the reduction of poverty, he puts forward the proposition that 'it is in culture that ideas of the future, as much as those about the past, are embedded and nurtured' (2002: 1). In the making of culture, a dialogue between 'aspirations' and 'sedimented traditions' takes place, which places futurity, rather than pastness, at the heart of our thinking about culture. He argues that empowering the poor in ways that enable people to advance their collective long-term interests in relation to wealth, equality and dignity, can be achieved through rethinking culture as 'the capacity to aspire'. By strengthening the capacity to have and to cultivate 'voice' through actions and performances which have local cultural voice, the poor can begin to change the 'terms of recognition' (Taylor 1992) with which they are invested by those in power. Appadurai claims that the poor operate with very weak resources where terms of recognition are concerned, and the challenge today in development work is how to bring the politics of dignity and the politics of poverty into a single framework. This book explores ways in which children creatively use language, images, objects, musical games, poems and performances as expressions of 'the capacity to aspire', and what this might mean for pedagogies within developing world contexts, such as South Africa.

Chapter 3

# How do I smile in writing?

## Transformations across modes

> How do you smile in writing?
> You attribute to letters a fortune that they cannot possess.
>
> Plato, Phaedrus

### Introduction

In Chapter 2 I outlined the key theoretical underpinnings to this research. In this chapter I demonstrate how using a social semiotic multimodal approach to analysing students' classroom texts can throw new perspectives on how students learn, and the implications of this for classroom practices.

This chapter is a case study discussion of the storytelling practices of one student, a 13-year-old Zulu-speaking girl, Lungile, who was called 'the silent one' by her teachers but turned out to be a gifted storyteller. Lungile was a student in the Grade 7 class involved in the Spruitview Storytelling Project, conducted in a primary school east of Johannesburg. This study of her storytelling practices in multiple modes, throughout the year, compares her use of different modes – multimodal performance, writing and image – to tell the 'same' story. Her uses of semiotic resources are intimately connected to her identity in the ways she draws on her individual socio-cultural history and the language practices of her home and wider community. Comparing her representations across modes gives us a better understanding of her transformations within and across modes. It also gives us insight into the variation and range of her meaning-making, demonstrating that her relationship to each mode is not the same: she inhabits each mode differently and uses the resources of each mode in different ways. I show how her different relations to and uses of modes produce different 'takes' on her narrative and therefore different forms and shapes of knowledge.

The chapter begins with a contextual overview of the Spruitview Storytelling Project, followed by an analysis of Lungile's multimodal storytelling performance. An analysis of how she represents the same story in writing and in drawing follows. I conclude with a discussion of the implications of this case study for multimodality and learning in diverse classrooms.

This chapter demonstrates how one can interpret students' multimodal texts using analytical tools developed from or based on multimodal social semiotics. The analysis of Lungile's visual text draws on Kress and van Leeuwen's *Grammar of Visual Design* (1996). In analysing Lungile's written text, I draw loosely on Halliday's *Introduction to Functional Grammar* (1985). However, in the case of Lungile's storytelling performances recorded on videotape, I have invented a framework. In each case, I make explicit the analytical framework used for the data analysis.

## The Spruitview Storytelling Project: background

In 1994, during the year of the first democratic elections in South Africa, I was fortunate to work with a Grade 7 class of boys and girls in a recently established primary school on the outskirts of Johannesburg. There were about 700 children in the school, most of whom lived in the nearby townships of Vosloorus and Thembisa. Although the school was situated in a suburban lower middle class neighbourhood, the majority of children came from unemployed or low income families.

There were 34 boys and girls in this class, varying in age and ability. Most of them were 12 or 13 years old but there were 5 boys aged 16 who had missed out on years of consistent schooling due to the political violence in the 1980s. All the children were multilingual, fluent in at least three South African languages. The languages spoken in the class included Zulu, Sotho, Venda, Swazi and Afrikaans. English was spoken as a home language by 10 per cent of the class. At the time, the Grade 7 students were learning all their content subjects through the medium of English, as well as learning three languages as subjects: English and Afrikaans, the official languages of that time, as well as a third language, Zulu or Sotho, which may or may not have been a home language for individual children. Following official language-in-education policy at the time, the medium of instruction up to the fifth year of schooling was an African language. These children had switched to using English as medium in Grade 5, i.e. two grades earlier (see Macdonald 1990; Hartshorne 1992; De Klerk 1995, 2002; Heugh *et al.* 1995; Granville *et al.* 1998; Heugh 2002; Bloch and Alexander 2003 on the history of South Africa's language-in-education policy). In the teaching of English as a subject, the English-only model was dominant, even though children were continuously code-switching in group and pair work. Written work in English was required in South African Standard English, with a heavy emphasis on correctness. Notices in the classrooms and around the school urged children to speak English as much as possible. It is important to point out that the only context in which these children encountered an attempt at linguistic purity was in their grammar classes at school. Outside of school, they were immersed in a densely cosmopolitan, urban environment in the economic heartland of the country, where multilingualism was the norm. One child, reflecting afterwards on the multilingualism in the Storytelling Project said:

> Outside the school we mix languages, then we come into school and there's Sotho and Zulu. But in this class, we can use all our languages, it's a classroom without walls.

## Aims of the project

The main aim of the Spruitview Storytelling Project was to provide a free space for the children to produce a body of stories which could be compiled into a class booklet of local stories. I was interested in creating a pedagogic environment which would encourage children to draw on the multi-semiotic communicative practices of their everyday lives outside of formal schooling. The focus was on their uses of narrative genres in playgrounds, homes, streets and communities. Multilingualism was central to the production of these narratives.

In order to facilitate the process of multilingual storytelling, the children were given the following task:

1 Divide yourselves into language groups where you all speak the same language/s.
2 Each person in the group tells a story. The story can be a story you have heard from someone in your family or community or a story you make up yourself. Tell the story in the language/s it was told to you.
3 Translate the stories, if necessary, so that everyone understands.
4 Choose the best stories in the group to tell to the rest of the class.
5 As a class, listen to the best stories from each group. Storytellers should introduce their stories by telling the audience where and when they heard the story. Storytellers should tell the story in the language in which it was told to them, and use translators to translate the story into English.
6 After each storytelling event, talk about some of the different meanings the story has for you. Discuss why you think the story was told.
7 When you have finished, write the story in the language in which it was told and translate it into English.
8 Draw the story.

The project took a year to complete, working with the class for one hour a week. By the end of the year, the class had produced a body of over 100 stories in different languages, genres and modes. What began as a fairly unstructured, rather chaotic activity became more and more focused as the children became more involved in their stories and the processes of telling them. Recordings of all the students' storytelling performances were made on video and shown to the students and interested teachers throughout the year.

The use of translation was central to this project. All the stories that were spoken or written in languages other than English were translated by the students into English. This focused students' attention on the linguistic resources required for communicating their meanings accurately for an audience. In several cases, they went home to ask members of their households to assist them in these translations. They formed peer groups of 'translation' services. Through these interactions, students engaged in meta-reflections about language and its potential that could only increase their linguistic knowledge and awareness of the differences between their home languages and English. They began to indulge in creative forms of language play in the translation of their stories. In their performances, they used translation as a communicative resource and a comic device. The audience took it upon themselves to participate in these acts of translation, demonstrating the extent to which translation was part of their everyday lives. Multilingual jokes were hugely popular and many were about the creativity of language. Here are some examples of the children's multilingual puns where words and phrases sound similar across languages but have absurd meanings:

> Do you see a cat? (English) – dunusani nginikethe (Zulu)
> **Bend so that I can choose you/Show me your arse.**
>
> Mediterranean sea (English) – Mee (Sotho) tereni (Zulu) yansiya (Sotho)
> **Mother, the train is leaving me.**
>
> Jesus is coming alone (English) – Morena jeso uganyilwe ke alone (Sotho)
> **Lord Jesus is choked by aloe.**
>
> Mango Sutho Buthelezi (Zulu name) – Mango wabasotho otheletsi (Zulu)
> **The Sotho mango is a sangoma concoction.**
>
> Peter Stuyvesant (English name) – Peter le steve balwanela sente (Sotho)
> **Peter and Steve are fighting for a cent.**

At the end of the project the written stories, jokes and drawings were collected together in a booklet called:

> *Our Stories in Our Languages/Dipale tsa rona ka leleme la rona/Dinaane tsa rona ka leleme la rona/Ngano dzashe nga nyambo dzashe/Amabali ethu angelwimi zethu/Dikanegelo tsa polelo ya geso/Tindzaba tetfu ngetilwimi tetfu/Switori swa hina hi tindzimi ta hina/Izindaba zethu ngamalimi wethu/Ons stories in onse tale: A Multilingual Collection of Stories, Jokes and Drawings.*

Each student in the class, as well as every teacher in the school, was given a copy of the book. When asked to comment on making the book, one student said:

> Collecting our stories and putting them together into one book was so important. It united us, it brought us together . . . from many things, we made one thing.

## The stories themselves

The range of genres produced by the children and understood within the broad category of 'story' included well-known folkloric tales *(dinonwane),* contemporary political satirical stories, jokes, radio advertisements and jingles, comic radio and rap routines, rap songs, dramatised dialogues and storytelling performances. Approximately one third consisted of narratives in the genre of folkloric tales (*dinonwane*). Some of these were transformations of these tales in response to the political moment, what I call the Political Tales. Most of the folkloric tales the children told were based on well-known trickster stories with animal characters, principally Hare and Lion. The small hare is the most successful trickster in African folklore and uses a combination of guile and wit to outsmart his opponents, who are usually bigger and stronger than himself. Stories produced in this genre included titles such as, 'Rabbit and Delivery Man', 'Hare and Tortoise', 'Rabbit, Lion and other Animals', 'Lion Skin and Rabbit', 'Nogqaza', 'Hare and Lion' and 'Inganekwane'. Other stories presented in the category of *dinonwane* were African versions of well-known tales such as 'Nwako and the Giant' ('Jack and the Beanstalk'), 'Red Jersey and the Jackal' ('Little Red Riding Hood') and 'Five Indian Brothers'. Other tales included 'Tselane and the Giant', 'The Wisdom Bird', 'The Hawks and the Hen', 'Grandmother and Grandfather', 'The Bride, the Bridegroom and the Old Woman' and 'The Two Brothers and their Grandmother'. A number of stories involved cannibals: 'Tselane and the Giant', 'Zantatoza', 'The Monster who Ate People', 'Grandmother and Grandfather', 'The Boy Sankatana', 'The Story of Apole' and 'Ngwako's Story'. Some of these stories are discussed in detail in Chapter 4.

The most popular genres with the audience were the Political Tales and the Jokes. The Political Tales were contemporary, satirical, politicised versions of tales from the canon of folkloric 'traditional' stories. These stories had as their central characters high-profile political leaders of the current time, including Nelson Mandela, leader of the main liberation party, the ANC; F.W. de Klerk, leader of the ruling apartheid Nationalist party; P.W. Botha, previous leader of the Nationalist Party; and Gatsha Buthelezi, leader of the Inkatha Freedom Party, an ethnically based 'Zulu' party from Kwa-Zulu Natal. In these Political Tales, political leaders (sometimes disguised as animals) connive to outwit one another to gain political power. These transformed versions of the well-known *dinonwane* were circulating in local homes and streets. The most popular Political Tale was a story about De Klerk, Botha and Mandela told by the class joker. It is a reworking of older versions of Hare and Lion trickster tales. The story was originally told in Sotho:

> There was Botha, De Klerk and Mandela. De Klerk was very rich and Mandela was his garden boy. One day De Klerk said to Mandela, 'Cook a chicken nicely for I am going to call Botha to have supper with us.' Mandela started cooking. In the process he became hungry, then he took a chicken's thigh. The thigh was very delicious. He ate the whole chicken and left the bones. De Klerk came back with Botha ready to enjoy the chicken. He said to Mandela, 'Bring the chicken to the table so that we can enjoy it.' Mandela said to De Klerk, 'Before you eat the chicken, go and sharpen a knife which you will use when you eat.' De Klerk went out to sharpen his knife. While De Klerk was out sharpening his knife, Mandela went to Botha and said, 'Botha, De Klerk is sharpening a knife to kill you, you must run away. Before you do so you need to smear some fat around your lips.' Botha did as he was told. When De Klerk came back, Mandela said to him, 'Look, Botha is running away with your chicken. Run after him!' De Klerk chased Botha for his chicken. He caught him and asked, 'Why do you run away with my chicken?' Botha said, 'What chicken? Mandela told me to run away because he said you want to kill me!'

Mandela, the lowly 'garden boy', is the trickster, who, through various forms of cunning, outwits his white masters, manipulating them into turning on one another while he runs off with the spoils (the chicken). The story works at many levels: as a metaphor for the overthrow of the ruling classes by the workers, for acts of resistance against colonial masters, for the political actions of black South Africans 'boys' taking control over their white 'masters' in April 1994. It also describes the ways in which Mandela, through a mixture of wisdom, connivance and political acumen, outwitted the white ruling party Nationalists to become the first president in a democratic South Africa. The tale plays in interesting ways with the trope of the 'garden boy' in relation to Mandela. In the early 1960s, during the Rivonia period when Mandela was on the run from the apartheid government, he disguised himself as a 'garden boy' named David on the Rivonia farm, tricking people into believing that he was simply the 'garden boy'. At the same time, he was leading the resistance movement and plotting the violent overthrow of the South African state. So the idea of the 'poor' Mandela leading the 'rich' white leadership a merry dance as he does in this story, is close to the actual truth of what was happening before he was caught in 1964 and subsequently jailed for 27 years. Today, a photo of Mandela during his imprisonment on Robben Island captioned 'A prisoner working in the garden', taken by the prison authorities, forms the centrepiece of the Mandela Prison Archive.

## Lungile's stories

One of the most gifted performing storytellers in the class was Lungile, a 13-year-old girl from a Zulu-speaking family. Initially quite shy, she was encouraged to tell stories by her friends and gained more and more confidence in her performances over the year. She had a strong sense of the comic and enjoyed telling political jokes, which she did with a great deal of charm. In the rest of this chapter, I focus on one story she told, called *Madevu Mbopha*, which was her first and longest story. I examine how she translates and transforms this same story into storytelling performance, writing and image.

Lungile's performances are all body. That is to say, that her use of her body – her smile, her use of her hips and torso, her specific click sounds, her eye movements – all work together to animate her meanings. As she moves through her performances, she is clearly drawing on a repertoire of representational resources which are deeply familiar to her and which she chooses to use. These resources can be loosely characterised within the performance conventions, genres and themes associated with African oral storytelling, which has existed in Southern African communities for generations in multiple forms and contexts (Scheub 1975; Hofmeyr 1994). When interviewed about how she acquired her oral storytelling practices, Lungile recounted how she had learnt how to tell stories through her interactions with her late grandmother, in a form of intergenerational apprenticeship:

> Every evening she told me this story. I lived with her. She is late. I was ten years old when she started telling me this story. She told it to me in Zulu. One day she told it to my brother and my mother. She sat in a chair and we sat on the floor. We used to watch TV at 8 then about 8.30 she told me stories. She told me three stories, this one and another two . . . She knew these stories. I just listened to these stories, then I went to sleep. She told me in Zulu, not the Zulu I know which is not the real Zulu . . . In Natal, they talk that real Zulu . . . I can't speak that real Zulu.

Scheub (1975), in his classic study of *ntsomi* performances by Xhosa women, describes them as involving 'much more than the word'. It is not the plot that is of primary interest to the audience; it is the performance that counts. *Ntsomi* performances are indeed, 'much more than the word'. Such events are fundamentally multimodal in their multilayered combination of language, sound, space, the visual, the gestural and movement of the whole body. Scheub describes this multimodality in terms of 'the language' of the artistic performance:

> The 'language' of this artistic performance involves much more than the word. It includes the relationship with the audience, the nuance of

> the hand, the movement of a hip, the subtlety of the face, the range and variety of human sounds, the rhythmic use of language; it includes a physical touch, a sudden and fleeting bit of mime, a dancing-in-place. It includes the music of the word that occasionally flows into song, the arrangement of detail, episode, and plot within a broader narrative context, the manipulation of surface plots to create profound themes. It involves the blending of gesture and word, of dance (body movements) and song, so that they become so closely interwoven that is it impossible to speak of one without treating the other. The performance depends on a repertory of images common to both artist and audience, so that there is a constant understanding and enticing of images flowing between the two entities
>
> (Scheub 1975: 14–15)

What follows is an extract from Lungile's story, *Madevu Mbopha* which shows the multimodality of her performance text: how meaning is being made 'everywhere, in every layer' in her communicational ensemble (Kress and Van Leeuwen 2001). The performance theorist Phelan (1993) has noted the difficulty of writing about performance: how does one write about live performance, whose only life is in the present? Describing it in writing changes its status, shape and meaning. Given the limitations of a written description of such an event, the extract below consists of a transcript of the verbal narrative text performed in Zulu, followed by an English translation. The transcript is accompanied by a metacommentary on her performance, highlighting aspects of its multimodality. The purpose of this commentary is to demonstrate how Lungile draws on different semiotic resources and to highlight the different semiotic layerings that are occurring from moment to moment. A number of 'freeze frames' taken from the videotext of her performance accompany this commentary (Figs 3.1, 3.2, 3.3). Each frame captures a particular moment in the performance. These freeze frames provide the reader/viewer with essential information on Lungile's position in the space, her posture, her use of eye contact and gaze direction, arm and torso movements, facial expressions and smile. Each frame is accompanied by a slice of the verbal narrative which was part of that moment.

## The challenges of transcription

Multimodal transcription poses enormous challenges. Any kind of transcription is an interpretive and transformative process, where richly textured data is reduced for the purposes of analysis: as such the mode of data presentation is a sign of the 'subjectivity' of the researcher and the research aims (Flewitt 2006). Norris (2004) has noted that multimodal transcription is a constant interplay between analysis and method of description. Each mode in a communicative event takes on equal weight and spoken language has the status of one mode in a host of others. Transcribing video data is a laborious, time-consuming task which has be managed step-by-step. Flewitt has classified video data as 'dynamic visual text' to reflect the temporal, spatial and kinaesthetic nature of visually recorded interaction, as well as the 'multilevelled interpretive process of the researcher, participants and readers' (Flewitt 2006: 35). A major challenge of transcription involves 'translating' the visual and audio aspects into a written format. How do you describe in language a particular gesture or body movement which captures a sense of the visual image? In the case of the storytelling performance captured on video, it was complicated by the fact that Lungile told the performance in Zulu. A Zulu transcript had to be made of the linguistic text, and then translated into English. It was necessary to begin the data analysis with a small segment of the performance and first categorise the different modes which were present in the performance, for example, gesture, language, sound and body movement. This involved many hours of watching the videotaped performance, with and without sound. It also involved working with 'cultural informants' who could explain, for example, the meaning of Lungile's special use of the click sound at certain key moments in the performance. Then the use of each mode had to be described separately. Once this had been accomplished, it was necessary to see how the different modes were in sequential and simultaneous dialogue and juxtaposition, and how they were producing meaning across the whole text.

The commentary below of a fragment of Lungile's videotaped performance is an analysis and description of what she is doing moment by moment in her performance. Field notes provided aspects of the event which could not be captured on video. The commentary provides a broad picture, focusing on what appeared to be salient at the time in the videotext. This also assumes that the videotext is not neutral but a selective text in itself, where certain aspects of the performance have been focused on for recording, and not others. The analysis and descriptive commentary draws on the following categories of description, which have been imposed on the videotext performance:

- the use of spoken language (varieties of Zulu, including standard Zulu);
- the use of sound (at the level of pitch, tone, inflections of dialogue of specific characters);
- the use of rhythm and pace ;
- the use of eye contact and gaze;
- the use of the mouth;
- the use of the smile;
- the use of laughter;
- the use of the hips;
- the use of the upper body (torso);
- the use of arms and hand movements;
- the use of the whole body in movement;
- interactions with and orientations to and away from the audience.

## Synopsis of *Madevu Mbopha*

Madevu Mbopha and Tall Man are leaders of two different communities. The story tells of their rivalry and destructive struggle for power over resources (frogs, sheep, cattle, fish, houses and gold) and people. In the end, it is Madevu's own dissatisfied people who strangle him to death and institute Tall Man as their new king. However, Tall Man falls victim to their wrath and is held by the throat until he dies. After the death of these two tyrants, 'everything became visible' and 'people led a happy life'. The story can be read as an allegory of the power of ordinary people to overthrow tyranny and corruption, and how after this action, new hopes and possibilities are made visible.

*The class is chattering noisily as Lungile walks to the front of the class. She takes up her place on the imaginary stage and shyly waits. She makes no eye contact with the audience seated on the floor in front of her. She waits. The class settles into stillness. She turns her head and fixes her eyes on the audience and smiles. It is the opening gesture, the generic feature that establishes her connection to her viewers and listeners. But hers is not a smile of confidence. It is tentative, revealing her state of nervousness, shyness and uncertainty. It is not a smile with the audience, or at the story material. It sets up a promise for what is to come; it seduces her audience into attentiveness, and at the same time, establishes a key bodily resource that she draws on to communicate. She intuits the stillness as her cue to start speaking. She begins speaking softly: in a low pitch and low volume. Her speaking pace is rapid, she swallows her words. She is nervous, unsure of where her audience is. Are they with her yet? As she speaks, her tone is serious and subdued:*

> Lendaba engizoyixoxa ngaxoxelwa ugogo wami. **The story I am going to narrate was told by my grandmother to me.**

*At the mention of her grandmother, her tone is respectful, the volume low. She pauses for a moment. With her hands, she nervously tucks in her jersey. She is beginning to use her hands as another important resource to communicate her meanings. She continues to speak quietly:*

> Ugogo wami ngelinye ilanga wangitshela ukuthi – **One day my grandmother told me that –**

*Her tone and mood begin to change. She raises her volume and pitch. The tone lightens up; she introduces a moment of jest and humour. She continues to make eye contact with the audience and begins smiling as she looks at them:*

> kwakukhona enye indoda – Madevu Mbopha – **There once lived a man called Madevu Mbopha, known as the bearded one –**

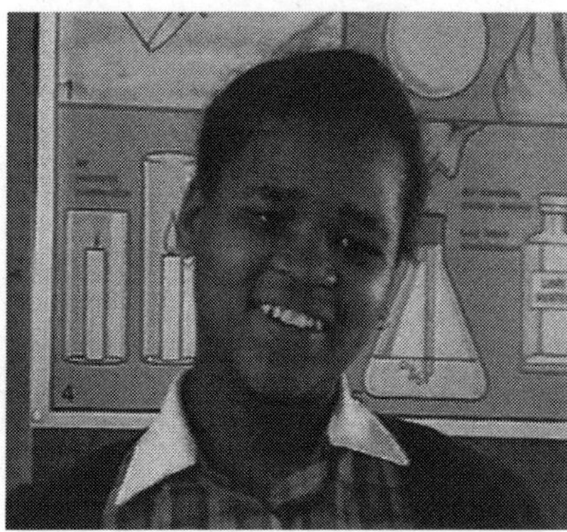

*Figure 3.1*
Multimodal performance of *Madevu Mbopha* by Lungile: 'There once lived a man called Madevu Mbopha . . .

*At the first mention of the name of the main character in the story, she fixes her lips in a smile, but this smile is different, indicating a different interest: she seems to be signifying to her audience how the name should be received. Through this transformation, she signals a move out of herself and into her role as storyteller. As she smiles at the story material with the audience, the particular comic shape and movement of her lips causes the audience to break out into laughter. She uses this feedback as a productive resource: she laughs with them, in the knowledge that she has won them round in the first few minutes but could lose them any minute. This laughter frees her from her nervousness and she is now poised to set the story afloat, to set it galloping. From now on, throughout this event, she chooses to laugh at something before the audience does. She recognises that she needs to engage in two ways with her audience in this communication: at the level of representation, and in relation to the message for communication to her audience. Laughing before her audience does communicate particular messages to them in an act of irony and self-reflexivity that positions her within and outside of the performance. Such a feature of the performance can work to build solidarity between her and her audience, helping to pull her audience together into one mass. She pauses for a moment then continues speaking with a fuller volume, a more confident tone:*

> Kwakuyinkosi yalapha la kade bahlala khona ayi – **He was the king of the area that was inhabited by people – now let me tell you what happened next –**

*This is the first introduction of the exclamation, 'ayi', which she continues to use regularly through the twelve-minute performance. 'Ayi' is untranslatable in English. It means a combination of 'and then'/'now let me tell what happened' and is used as a linguistic and sound resource throughout this story to keep the audience in suspense and to encourage prediction and anticipation. However, it is not only a word but also a particular exclamatory sound that has a phatic force. Lungile uses it as a sound that links together her narrative. It becomes her 'signature', which she uses regularly to create movement in the story and to amuse her audience. The first time she uses this signature, the audience break out in laughter in response to the particular ironic inflection she gives to this sound-word: her use of pitch, volume and tone is sharp, high and playful. In her use of this sound-word, Lungile is importing a sign from another domain of provenance: she is working with this sound-word which was used by her grandmother in her own versions of this tale. But Lungile does not 'imitate' or 'reproduce' her grandmother's inflection patterns. Rather, she challenges her grandmother's authority publicly by providing a playful parody and ironic gloss on her grandmother's use. In this choice, she establishes another interesting shift of distance and innovation in her telling of the tale. The teenage audience laugh knowingly in response to her irony – a gesture that simultaneously honours and distances herself from her grandmother's generation. In this transformation, she draws on the resources of her culture, her history and the communicative moment of the present to shape her own individual performance:*

> - labantu laba aba . . . khona bekuhlala abantu abafishane abangaka –
> **Those people, the ones that were there, were short people, this high –**

*The phrase 'labantu laba aba -' is incomplete. She does not say the word 'short people' fully but decides in the middle of the word 'aba' to change direction thematically and syntactically and to start with the concept of place, not the people. So she says, 'The ones that were there were short, this high' accompanied by a hand and eye gesture. There are a number of explanations possible for this thematic switch, which becomes a form of creative reshaping: inexperience which becomes knowledge halfway through the thought as she realises that it is more effective for her communicative purposes at this point to foreground a sense of place. It also gives her time to place the emphasis on the description of the people as 'short', which she indicates with a series of hand gestures, bringing the moment alive in a comic way. At the mention of the adjective 'abangaka' which means 'so high' she moves her right shoulder slightly and in a sophisticated series of bodily movements, she indicates with a hand gesture the word 'so high' but her eyes do not follow her hand gesture: they remain fixed on the audience, staying with them. Later on, in a kind of painting in the air, she uses a series of gestures to depict the two 'tall men' using both her hands followed by a gaze towards the ceiling for each one. Thus for the concept of 'short' and 'tall' she uses gesture and eye contact to help the audience visualise the height of the characters – a key theme in the story.*

*It is at the point of mentioning the two tall men that she gestures with both her arms and takes the visual and gestural representation of the story in space onto a different spatial level. Up until this point, she has limited the gestures spatially to her eye level but with the mention of the two tall men, she introduces another dynamic of height through raising her arms above this level and using her eyes to look upwards. By doing this, she is extending the imaginative and visual world of the story for the audience beyond the limits of her own body:*

> Bonke kade bebafishane. Kunomunye umuntu omude . . . ayi noMadevu Mbopha kade amude. Kade bayi-two akade babade – ayi – **All his people were short with the exception of one man who was tall . . . now let me tell you what happened, Madevu was also tall, there were only two tall people, now let me tell you what happened –**

*In this section she elaborates and emphasises two key concepts of shortness in the community and tallness in the two leaders. In her mention of both these terms she continues to use hand and eye gestures to indicate the physical differences in height. At the same time she remembers to repeat at regular timed intervals, her signature 'ayi' to keep her audience in the palm of her hand, which at this point they still are, laughing each time with her at her inflection of the word 'ayi'. In terms of the linguistic resources available to her, she has an extended repertoire consisting of elements from different domains: she draws on varieties of Zulu, including deep Zulu and township Zulu. She draws on English, for example, in her use of the numeral 'two' in 'bayi-two':*

> Manj' uMadevu Mbopha bekuyinkosi – ayi – UMadevu Mbopha abantu bakhona athi, 'Man! Imvula mayinetha nonke nibaleke ningene endlini' Ayi, bambheka bambheka bathi – **Now Madevu Mbopha as he was king, now let me tell you what happened – Madevu Mpopha told his people, 'If it rains, all of you must enter your houses quickly' . . . Now let me tell what happened, they looked at him and they looked at him and said . . .**

*Maintaining the use of the word-sound, 'ayi' as a key resource, she now activates different performance elements within her repertoire: role-play and the use of direct speech. Keeping her gaze on the audience, she role-plays the king's command through direct speech and simultaneously attempts to project the idea of this character through taking on the stature and the tone of the king. The shift in pitch, volume and tone is slight but significant to signal flexibility with performance genres. In becoming the king, she lifts her shoulders, puffed up in a symbolic gesture of power, places her lips in a fixed position and then begins to speak. It is interesting to notice how her body movements always precede her spoken language: in her performances, she uses her body in distinctive ways to convey states of feeling and emotion which language cannot do. In her role-play of the king, she takes on the gestures, tone and volume without irony.*

*Her use of repetition in, 'They looked at him and they looked at him . . .' is one of the features of spoken language and a defining feature of African oral storytelling. It is an important resource in performance, which buys the performer time as she thinks on her feet, but more importantly, enables the audience to follow the content and rhythms of the story. It is at this point that Lungile falters. She starts: 'Now let me tell what happened, they looked at him and they looked at him and said . . .' What they said never emerges from her mouth. However, in an action of creativity and imagination, she swiftly abandons one direction, switches to another*

*Figure 3.2*
Multimodal performance of *Madevu Mbopha* by Lungile: 'All these people were short with the exception of one man who was tall . . .

*and introduces new information about the protagonists. It is in moments of rupture like these that we see how the making of signs is a constant process of remaking, guided by the interests of the sign-maker in the communicative moment:*

> 'Mm! Lomuntu lona omude wayeyenza ukuthi imvula ine. Kade batshelene noMadevu Mbopha. Enza ukuthi imvula ine ishaye kakhulu izindlu ziphephuke. Ayi! Manje kade kade kune lakuhlala khona izimvu. Lapho obekuhlala khona izimvu esibayeni sezimvu. Ayi – Wasuko lapho uMadevu Mbopha manje . . . imvula ine kakhulu . . . imvula ine . . . ine kakhulu. Ayi! Abantu bagijima bangena endlini. Ine imvula ishaye izindlu zonke zilale phansi izindlu zonke. Abantu bazivale ngengubo. Bathathe amasenke bazivale ngawo. **The Tall man was the rainmaker. There was a lot of collaboration between him and Mbopha about rain making. The Tall man used to make heavy rains. These rains were accompanied by strong winds which used to blow the houses away . . . Now let me tell you what happened – Madevu then moved away. It rained heavily. It rained for a long time. Now let me tell you what happened . . . The people ran into their houses. The rain continued; it demolished all their houses. The people covered themselves with blankets. They made shelters with 'zincs'.**

*In this section, the first important plot event takes place in the form of the devastating storm, which destroys everything. Lungile's energy levels increase dramatically as she provides a graphic and densely animated description of the moments of the storm, through the repetition of references to the rain and the details of the people's responses to it. As she describes the storm, she uses the full range of her bodily resources – her arms and hands, hips, torso, legs, head, eyes and facial features, to give life to and convey the atmosphere of the storm. She puts her hands over her head to show people running for cover, she mimes people gathering blankets and covering themselves. There is a softening of the voice; her pitch and volume decrease as she tells of people covering themselves in blankets under their shacks of corrugated tin. Her use of the term 'amasenke' is the Sotho term for 'zincs', the term for corrugated tin sheets which people use to make shacks. This is another example of how she uses linguistic resources she knows her audience are familiar with:*

> Bafike labantu abafishane. Kukhona labantu abafishane kade basebenzela lomuntu lo omude. Bafike namabhakede. Bafike na . . . kade kukhone indawo . . . kade kuse kusemfuleni kunamafishi mhlawumbe kune lona . . . ixoxo zonke zihlala khona lapho. Mabafika khona bafika namabhakede baikhiphe bathi kunamofishi. Bakhiphe amafish bakhiphe amafishi emabhakadeni. Bawakhiphe bawafake emabhakedeni. **Then the short people who had been working for the tall man arrived . . . They came along with buckets. They came there, there was a place, and it was a river that was teeming with fishes and frogs, the whole lot. On their arrival there, they took out all the fish from the water. They filled their buckets with fish. They filled the buckets with fish . . . they filled the buckets with fish . . . they filled the buckets.**

*Her tone, pitch and volume shifts again with the next major plot event: the looting of fish from the river. She drops the volume, drops the energy levels, picking it up briefly as she describes the looting process. As she describes the servants of the tall man-thief storming into the village and stealing the fish, her whole body starts to sway a movement that is primarily located in her hips. Her body bends as the dwarfs take the fish out of the river and put them into the buckets. The force and pace of this activity is displayed through her swaying body, which enacts the movements of picking up and bending down, from the torso. Her voice deepens and the repetition of the lines picks up the pace and rhythm of the activity. As the tension and activity in the village increases, so do her body movements. They seem almost unconscious because they are so flawless, so practised, but these body movements that she draws upon are deeply rooted. Lungile demonstrates a deep socio-cultural and historical knowledge of those particular 'ways with the body', having moved in these ways many times before.*

In the above commentary on Lungile's performance, I have tried to illustrate how her meaning is made in multiple ways, at multiple levels and places, in different modes and media, drawing on different domains of provenance. Lungile is drawing on the resources of spoken language, space, gesture, narrative and vocalisation. Her use of these resources, however, is not innate or natural, rather they have become naturalised and developed through

*Figure 3.3*
Multimodal performance of *Madevu Mbopha* by Lungile: 'It rained heavily. It rained for a long time. The people ran into their houses . . .'

constant exposure to the practice within her cultural community. Her individual development needs to be understood within a socio-cultural-historical theory which assumes that individual development constitutes and is constituted by social and cultural-historical activities and practices (Rogoff 2003). Thus her performance forms part of the history of the practice, the ongoing semiotic chain. Although her use of language is central to her story, it cannot be separated from how she uses her whole body to provide a living, dynamic performance.

Lungile's performance is gendered. She has been taught how to please her audience, to use her body as a charm. She pouts, she smiles, she disengages, she seduces. Phelan (1993: 150) has noted that for performance art, the referent is always the 'agonisingly relevant body of the performer'. Lungile has learnt how to move her hips and sway in culturally defined ways, which are at times sexual, and at times, how women move when performing ordinary everyday tasks. One of these culturally defined hip movements is to disarticulate her torso from her hips so that her hips are moving almost independently of the rest of her body. This is a common use of the hips in traditional African women's dances. She continues to sway throughout her performances in a ritualistic way and to move her hands to convey the gestures of the characters in the speech. In her use of eye contact with her audience, she avoids it initially – making eye contact in some African communities is a sign of disrespect. However, as a relationship develops with the audience, she uses it to her advantage, withdrawing and maintaining it when she senses the need or power.

The feminist philosopher, Butler, problematises the materiality of the body in relation to gender and sex, arguing that the body is always an 'embodying of possibilities both conditioned and circumscribed by historical convention'. She argues that the classification of bodies into the categories of male or female in Western culture constructs 'gender' as a discursive practice that constitutes 'bodies' as sexed through a natural process:

> To do, to dramatise, to reproduce, these seem to be some of the elementary structures of embodiment. This doing of gender is not merely a way in which embodied agents are exterior, surfaced, and open to the perception of others. Embodiment clearly manifests a set of strategies, or what Sartre would perhaps have called a style of being or Foucault 'a stylistics of existence'. This style is never fully self-styled, for living styles have a history, and that history conditions and limits possibilities.
>
> (Butler 1990: 272)

This 'style of being' is manifest in all the performative acts which make up our social and material being: how we dress, adorn ourselves, use gesture, mark our bodies, inflect our language and accents, move and use our body in ritualised ways. Through the repetition of these acts of embodiment, our identities become constituted. Franks has noted how in improvised dramatic activity 'the body acts as a signifier' and the 'reiterated performative acts place the body as signifier in history and render it visible' (Franks 1996: 7).

Lungile's 'doing of gender' in her performance is an embodiment of a style of being, behaving and acting in accordance with cultural norms around what it means to inhabit 'femaleness' and 'female storyteller' identities. The style of her gendered body is infused with her own unique qualities, what she has learnt about the gendered body from her grandmother, her peers, the media and all the other influences which have shaped her sense of 'body'. She has at her disposal a repertoire of body movements to draw on. Thus I argue that none of her body movements in her performances are 'natural' – they are part of how her femininity has been shaped and stylised by the gendered power relations in which she is immersed. Her body is inscribed with her own unique inflections of these social and cultural markers, which simultaneously stamp her performance as 'female'.

## Lungile's written text

Iedema's term 'resemiotization' has been used to describe how within multimodal communication, 'meaning-making shifts from context to context, from practice to practice, or from one stage of a practice to the next' (2003: 40–1). Through such processes of resemiotisation, meaning-making becomes progressively rematerialised through different forms of material realisations. Such processes lead to forms of recontextualisation (Bernstein 1990: 60–192) in which situated and quite local forms of knowledge can become more and more reified through different processes of interaction and reshaping.

Lungile's shift across modes from performance to writing can be constructed as a form of resemiotisation which mobilises radically different spheres of human experience. Lungile's elaborated use of whole body movement is the central pivot around which her storytelling performance of Madevu Mbopha revolves. However, in the act of writing, her use of her body in time and space shifts dramatically. Writing involves a particular disciplining of the body (Foucault 1979; Luke 1992): redirecting the body into a certain fixed, concentrated position, focusing her eyes and using her hands in the particular physical movements that the act of writing words onto the page demands. The challenge for Lungile is how to transform 12 minutes of multimodal performance in real time into the permanence of writing. Some of these decisions involve questions such as, what does she do with her smile, which is so central to her charming engagement with her audience? How does she smile in writing? What does she do with those special 'ayi' click sounds that kept her audience in her power? The performance life is in the present; it cannot be remembered as it was told.

In comparing Lungile's multimodal performance and her written text, one of the key differences is in her management and control of *what is said* and *how it is to be taken*. Olsen has pointed out that the experienced reader and writer is conscious of the management of both content and force:

> The experienced reader can recognise the mind behind the writing and the mind of the putative reader that the writer has in mind. These two minds the reader must co-ordinate with his or her own. Subjectivity is the recognition that each of these minds may have a different perspective on the world.
>
> (Olsen 1996:256)

Austin's (1962) central insight in speech-act theory was that even the most neutral reports of facts have an illocutionary force as well as a propositional content. In other words, statements express both content and the speaker's attitude to that content, the latter of which shows how the content is to be taken or read. How the reader or listener actually interprets the content is another matter entirely. In Lungile's storytelling performance she has control in varying degrees of the content of her text, 'what is to be said', but significantly, she has more control of how what is said is 'to be taken'. This is evident in the way in which she orientates her performance towards her audience, shaping and manipulating her narrative in response to this developing, dynamic relationship. For example, her varied use of the exclamation, 'ayi', provides a living connection to her audience, indicating how the 'text is to be taken'. In her written text, however, this signature sound-gesture is lost – it completely disappears. The same can be said for her smile, the swaying movements of the hip, her use of eye contact and all the other body elements in which she invests so much of her storytelling.

The shift from the use of performance to written language is a resemiotisation at a number of levels. The move from face-to-face multimodal interaction with a living, breathing audience, involving the complex use of the body, to the solitary confrontation with a blank page, is a shift in contexts, materiality and communicative practices. Such a shift mobilises the 'self' differently, drawing on different kinds of emotions, knowledges and forms of human experience. It also means re-orientation to who is being addressed. I think that for Lungile, the shift from full body performance to the mode of written language involves a profound loss. In some ways, she has to give up her body to inhabit a space of dis-embodiment, which the activity of writing demands. This shift from the full presence of body in performance to the discrete use of the body in writing can be read as a movement from embodiment to forms of dis-embodiment, from forms of embedded, contextualised and situated shapes of knowledge to more abstract, reified forms. Writing produces compactness and permanence. But what writing gains in permanence, it loses in comprehensiveness. The history of writing in the Western world is an attempt to invent lexical and syntactical devices that can compensate for what is lost. And the history of reading becomes an attempt to master these clues and the hermeneutical devices that provide some indication of how the writer intended the text to be taken (Olsen 1996: 111). In the South African context, where the majority of people's preferred mode of communication is oral, the values, knowledges and uses attached to written and spoken language as resources for communication are fundamental to understanding and interpreting contemporary culture and communication. They are also critical in trying to understand how children navigate their way through schooling.

In comparing Lungile's written text of Madevu Mbopha to her performance text, her written text is highly reduced in comprehensiveness. It is a profound reshaping of the narrative. Could this be seen *as a loss of control* over how the Madevu text is to be taken, indicating some kind of struggle with the semiotic resources available to her? Or could this be seen as *a different kind of control* over how the text is to be taken? She writes one version in her home language, Zulu, which in itself may orientate her towards producing a certain kind of discursive style, and a translation of this version into English. In both versions, she pares down the complex descriptions, actions and interactions from the performance version into a recount of the main events in the plot, of who does what to whom. She reshapes her story to focus on action and the series of actions that lead to the death of the one chief. In the performance, the action is densely embedded in detailed descriptions of people and places but in the written version, much of the extraneous matter and description which give the live performance its texture and vitality, has been eliminated. An analysis of her verb choices using Halliday's (1985) functional grammar shows a focus on action, and the use of predominantly material processes of 'doing' or 'happening', rather than mental processes of feeling, thinking and perceiving or relational processes of attribution or identification. In the following analysis of the use of verbs in her written text, which she has translated into English, the verbs in **bold** are material processes, the verbs in *italics* are mental or behavioural process, the verbs underlined are relational or existential:

> One day there was a king uMadevu Mbopha. This king had a nation of short people and a lot of animals. He also had a best friend whom he *loved* very much. Umadevu ngibophe *loved* gold. His friend had gold he **told** his friend to **sell** him the gold with all the animals he had he **went** to his house. Because he was tall the whole nation was afraid of him. He **told** them that they should not **go out** at night as there would be thunder with his witchcraft he *knew* there would be thunder. The people **gathered** everywhere and only the animals **were left**. The regiment of the king's friend who **sold** him the gold **arrived.** They **took** all the animals as well as the fish and **put** in buckets and **left** the place dry without even fish in the water. The houses have **collapsed** it's dawn the children are **crying**. The houses are made of corrugated iron when they **woke up** they had **collapsed**. In the morning the king **woke up** and **called** his regiment and **asked** them where the animals were and they **said** that they do not *know.*

- Number of material verbs: 20;
- Number of mental/behavioural verbs: 4;
- Number of relational/existential verbs: 12.

In her performance version, she focuses on action in order to keep the narrative moving along and hold her audience, but she infuses it with repetitions, detailed descriptions and elaborations of the events. Here is an example of her account of the stealing of the fish by the regiment of the king's friend:

> Bakike labantu abafishane. Kukhona labantu abafishane kade basebenzela lomuntu lo omunye. Bafike namabhakede. Bafike na . . . kade kukhone indawo . . . kade kuse kusemfuleni kunamafishi mhlawumbe kune lona . . . ixoxo zonke zihlala khona lapho. Mabafika khona bafika namabhakede baikhiphe bathi kunamofishi. Bakhiphe amafish bakhiphi amafishi ebhakedeni. Bawakhiphe bawafake emabhakedeni. Bathathe amaxoxo. Abanye baphathe amaxoxo. Bahambe namaxoxo. Bathathe nezimvu. Nezinkomo bathathe nayi-everything. Bathathe bahambe nayo. Ekuseni bathole kungena niks. Komile la akuna niks, akuna niks. Kusele ifishi eyi-one emanzini. Kusele ifishi eyi-one.
> **Then the short people who had been working for the tall man arrived . . . They came along with buckets. They came there, there was a place, it was a river that was teeming with fishes and frogs,**

> **the whole lot. On their arrival there, they took out all the fish from the water. They filled their buckets with fish. They filled the buckets with fish . . . they filled the buckets with fish . . . they filled the buckets. Some took the frogs out. They carried the frogs away. They also took the sheep away. The cattle were also taken away. They took everything. Then they went away. In the morning the people who lived there found absolutely nothing. The place was empty, there was nothing, niks. Except one fish left in the water. Only one fish.**

Compare the above version with her compacted written account:

> They **took** all the animals as well as the fish and **put** in buckets and **left** the place dry without even fish in the water.

A central question these two versions raise is: why didn't she elaborate more fully on the stealing of the fish in her written version of the story? It does not seem to be a question of her communicative competence: she has the competence to do so, as evident in her performance version, *but she has chosen not to use these resources*. Contrary to accepted theories on the importance of talking your way into writing in developing writing competence, Lungile's talking/performing her way into writing has not produced extended writing.

Halliday (1989) argues that written and spoken language are different but related languages and their distinctive characteristics vary according to their contexts and purposes of use. Written language presents a synoptic view of the world (world as product, as things, which can be attended to and analysed) and spoken language represents the world as 'happenings', dynamic processes that are always in flux. Written language is not simply spoken language written down. Writing is not anchored to the here-and-now, in the way that spoken language is.

It could be argued that Lungile's spoken performance powerfully captures the world as 'happenings' and dynamic processes which are shifting and changing and that her written version, 'They **took** all the animals as well as the fish and **put** in buckets and **left** the place dry without even fish in the water', is a synoptic view of the world as that which can be attended to and analysed. However, in the same way that Lungile's understandings of oral performance practices can be located within existing cultural forms outside of school, her understanding of writing culture in this context is defined by what counts procedurally and criterially as 'writing' institutionally. This happens at the macro level of policy and curriculum documents, and at the micro level of the school, and how specific teachers interpret and 'translate' these ideas into pedagogical practice.

Lungile is positioned as a participant in a much wider network of regulations around certain versions of literacy education in which what counts as 'writing' is tailored and modelled to fit the needs of the school and assessment system. As Freebody and Freiberg (2007) point out, these ideas about literacy perform powerful disciplinary and ideological work which has cultural consequences. Literacy education has institutional histories which are 'discursively produced as normative expectations,' against which teachers and ultimately 'whole communities' can be held accountable (2007: 7). Such ideas become invested with certain pedagogical techniques by individual teachers accompanied by a moral logic which gets played out in classroom practice.

Lungile's attitude and disposition in relation to writing has mainly been cultivated in school. Here is an example of another piece of her writing, which she wrote for her English teacher a month before she produced her piece of writing on Madevu Mbopha:

> A MEAL I REMEMBER
> My cousin asked me to a meal. It was Good Friday. They asked me because they were celebrating Good Friday. I eat at Dobsonville. It was 12 o'clock midday. There was my father, my mother as well as their children. We ate for one hour 15 minutes. We ate many kinds of food like turkey, ice cream and some snacks. The food tasted in their usual taste. Everyone liked the food because it tasted good. I remember this meal so well because it was a family meal. Yes I do think I will eat like this again because it was a Good Friday dinner.

The genre of this text is recount: it is an account of a particular event, a family meal, and focuses on the activities of various participants in this event. In its focus on action, this text is not very different from Lungile's written narrative on Madevu Mbopha. She has learnt that story writing involves writing a sequence of actions: this is how you produce written texts. Another feature of her performance text, which does not appear in her writing, is dialogue. Is this absence in her writing due to a struggle with mastery of the complexity of punctuation around writing direct speech, or is it because direct speech does not constitute 'writing'?

In *Learning to Write* (1994), Kress states that learning to write becomes the learning of the forms, demands and potentialities of different genres. Initiation into and mastery of the different disciplines is measured or constituted by the degree of mastery the individual has of the genres in which they are reported and written about and in which they exist:

> Hence the learning of the genres involves an increasing loss of creativity on the child's part, and a subordination of the child's creative abilities to the norms of the genre. The child learns to control the genre, but in the process the genre comes to control the child. Given the cognitive and social implications of these generic forms, the consequences for the child are immense.
>
> (Kress 1994: 11)

In her written text, Lungile's creativity is ever-present but she is learning to realise her creativity differently. She is in the process of learning to control the written genres of school, a process which requires a different relationship to her creativity she exercises in her multimodal performance. In the practice of writing, she mobilises different parts of herself and different aspects of her experience. Parts of herself are submerged; other parts are emerging, as she transforms herself from a 'performing person' into a 'writing person'. What we witness in these examples are some of the consequences of what happens when the genre begins to control the writer: the writer's relations to her creativity and to herself, are changed.

## Lungile's drawing

The final text Lungile created based on the narrative of Madevu Mbopha was a drawing in response to the task, 'Draw your story'. This two-dimensional drawing (Figure 3.4) was produced after she had completed both her multimodal performance and writing.

*Figure 3.4* Drawing of Madevu Mbopha by Lungile

The analysis draws on key aspects of Kress and Van Leeuwen's (1996) *Grammar of Visual Design*. The following main structures of the image are analysed:

- forms of representation;
- setting;
- appearance of the represented participants;
- composition;
- representation and interaction.

The purpose of the analysis is first, to gain some insight into how Lungile uses the mode of the two-dimensional image to realise her narrative; and second, to compare the different ways in which she uses performance, writing and drawing to shape and reshape her meanings.

## Forms of representation

Images can be either narrative or conceptual. The basic proposition in the narrative is representing the world in terms of 'doing' and 'happening'. Conceptual representations focus more on representing participants in terms of their classification, their generalised states of being or essences. Although Lungile's image is predominantly narrative in form, there are some conceptual elements in it as well. The narrative is in the visual depiction of a particular moment of violent conflict, in which the male figure on the right is throwing objects (perhaps stones or missiles) at another male figure on the left. What we are presented with is a dynamic moment of action, in which two men are involved in combative, aggressive behaviour, initiated by the male figure on the right in the role of Actor, (the one who initiates action), against the male figure on the left who is the Goal (the participant against which the deed of 'throwing' is instigated). The structure represented is therefore transactional as the relation between the two represented participants is depicted as a transaction, something done by one actor to a goal.

The key feature in a narrative representation is the presence of a vector. When a vector connects participants, they are represented as doing something to or for each other. These vectorial patterns are called narrative. Vectors are visible or invisible, strong diagonal lines. In this image there is a strong presence of a vector visibly inscribed on the image in the form of a line of arrows/stones running diagonally from the left hand of the male on the right towards the mouth of the opposite figure. The Actor is the participant from whom the vector departs: he is fused to the vector. The Goal is the participant at which the action is aimed. The visual structure of the arrows conveys a strong sense of the violence of the action through its careful targeting of the opponent.

The visible vector is accompanied by the direction of the glance of the male Actor. Action can also be in the form of a look known as a reaction process, in which a vector is formed by the direction of the glance of one or more of the participants. In this image the male on the right is represented as the active participant, the male opposite as the phenomenon at which the gaze is directed. The gaze of the two participants is bi-directional. Without the arrows providing the direction in this image, it would be unclear who is initiating the gaze. In terms of activity it is the right-hand male who is the aggressor.

Conceptual representations present participants in terms of their generalised, more or less stable and timeless essences, in terms of class, structures or meaning. Visual characteristics of the classification process in covert taxonomies include the use of symmetrical composition, in which participants are placed at equal distance from one another, given the same size and same orientation towards the horizontal and vertical axes. The background is plain and neutral; the angle is frontal and objective. Participants are often shown in a kind of decontextualised, objective way. This image, with its meticulous, detailed attention to the physical appearances of the two different male figures, in terms of their dress codes, hair styles and accessories, is also a covert classification of African male power, showing two styles of power in different domains. The man on the left is depicted as a traditional African chief, in all his costumed finery and attributes of symbolic power and status; the male figure on the right is recognisable as a particular style or 'type' of urban migrant mineworker, traditionally associated with deep-level mining on the Reef goldmines. His markers of identity are located in his black gumboots, his strong, naked torso, his shaven head and his ear wear. Conceptually, the image represents the tensions and struggles between traditional and modern forms of power, between the elite and the working class, between rural chiefdoms and industrialised labour. It also represents intergenerational rivalries and conflicts around masculinities – strong, virile youth who challenge the authority and power of the father.

### *Setting*

This action takes place in an abstract, undefined place, indicated by horizontal lines which are drawn rather roughly as 'scribbles' between the main figures and some spiral lines which frame the left and right outer edges of the drawing and which almost frame the male figures. Both male figures are foregrounded. This absence of a specific setting is significant; suggesting that for the artist, the drama between the two men takes place in an abstract, mythical setting disconnected from the 'real' world and that the energy of the drawing is focused on the two characters. It may also be that the concept of placing the characters in a 'setting' may not be familiar to the artist.

### *Appearance of participants*

The men are drawn with much attention to the details of their appearance, particularly their clothing, shoes, hairstyles, ear accessories and headgear. The kingliness of Madevu, on the left, is signified in a number of ways. He has not one, but two crowns, a small one perched near the front of his head and a larger one positioned over the back of his head. The small crown has a star in the middle, which may have religious significance referring to the African Zionist Churches who use a silver star symbol on their caps and on their clothing. The larger crown is similar in style to American Indian and African chief headdresses, which are often decorated with beautiful feathers. This crown is attached to a form of headpiece, similar in design to Egyptian wigs worn by kings and queens in ancient Egyptian relief paintings. Protruding from this wig over his forehead is a sharp object, perhaps a feather, as part of his headdress. These objects are often part of ancient Egyptian headdress, for example, the figure of an asp. He is wearing long, solid earrings and has shaved his beard into a particular style rather like lamb chops. He has a long, protruding nose, in contrast to the other male figure, which has a short, hawk-like nose.

Different styles of masculinity are depicted in the relationship between states of nakedness and dress. The tall man figure on the right has a naked torso and a shaven, 'naked' head. He carries the confidence of male youth in his physical beauty, prowess and strength. Madevu, on the other hand, embodies male symbolic power: he is clothed from head to foot in ornate markers of his status and power, carrying the weight of his position on his body.

The men's appearances display how their different identities are linked to different contexts of power. Madevu's clothes are an important marker of his symbolic power as chief. Drawing on Western, West African Yoruba and ancient Egyptian influences, Madevu is clothed from head to foot in a Western-style shirt with a collar and buttons all the way down the front. The highly elaborate sleeves are long with cuffs and they have either a striped pattern imprinted on them or they have been strip-woven in the style of West African kente cloth, in which expensive, traditional-style cloth is assembled from strips of silk or cotton material joined together into a patchwork. Madevu has multiple layers of clothing on his lower body, each layer signifying a particular affiliation and identity: the outer layer resembles a kind of skirt or a pair of wide culottes, which cover the underclothing and form the shape of a skirt. These kinds of skirt-culottes are part of the traditional design of clothing worn by West African royalty. The underneath layer of clothing is a pair of Western-style men's trousers. He is wearing short black boots.

The male figure opposite him, referred to in the story as 'tall man' and 'Madevu's friend' resembles, in appearance, young male migrant workers who come from neighbouring countries such as Lesotho and Mozambique or from rural areas in South Africa to work on the Witwatersrand gold mines. Gumboots are multiple signifiers in South Africa: apart from being associated in general with particular forms of industrial labour, they are associated with deep-level mining. Miners have to work up to their knees in water underground, in terrifying conditions of high temperatures, potential rock falls, gas poisoning, explosions, fire and dangerous machinery. Such work is highly dangerous and taxing to body and soul, but as Coplan points out in his study of male Basotho migrants who migrate from Lesotho to the South African mines, to go there is 'not only necessary, but manly, heroic' (Coplan 1994: 119). Youth, fitness, virility and courage are qualities that have become associated with the young men who have left their families to earn a living on the mines.

Gumboots are also associated with cultural forms – popular songs and sophisticated dances that miners have evolved on the mines as a form of entertainment. These dances are an art form, usually performed by highly athletic, fit males with naked torsos and shaven heads, wearing trousers tucked into their gumboots. These 'gumboot' dances consist of a complex combination of song and rhythmical dancing, in which co-ordinated stamping and slapping of the gumboots is central to the performance.

### *Composition*

Kress and van Leeuwen (1996) present three basic principles of composition: information value, salience and framing. Information value relates to where elements in the image are placed. For example, in cultures that read Roman scripts from left to right, elements to the left of the image encode information that is 'given' and to the right of the image information which is 'new'. In this image, the king Madevu is 'given' information and the tall man is 'new'. This makes sense in terms of the verbal text, in which the central character is Madevu and the antagonist is Tall Man. The position of the two participants is polarised, indicating their separateness and lack of connection. However, the linking element in the image is the travelling stone-arrow, which constitutes the relations between the two men and provides an explanation for the links between them.

Arrows can be used as semiotic resources to indicate relations between and among concepts (Kress *et al.* 2001). The arrows represent directionality, transactional processes and relational processes. In this image, the use of the arrows interspersed with small round objects, is a significant visual reference to express directionality, relational processes as well as intentionality. The arrows mixed with stones are a metaphor for the relationship of violence, rivalry and antagonism between these men. This relationship is made explicit through the directionality of the arrows, implying that the male on the right, the newcomer, is to blame for this violence. The use of arrows, at a more conceptual level, represents the relations between different forms of masculine power in an African setting.

### *Representation and interaction*

Images involve two kinds of participants: the *represented participants* who are the people, places and settings in the image itself, and the *interactive participants* who are the people who communicate with each other through images – the producers and the viewers of images. Interactive participants are therefore real people who make images and make sense of images in different social contexts. There are three kinds of relations between represented participants and interactive participants:

1 relations between the represented participants;
2 relations between interactive and represented participants;
3 relations between interactive participants.

In this image, the characters do not look at us, the viewers, but at one other. Their drama is being enacted in a closed world, and the viewer is a spectator to this event. In terms of its interactive meaning, the picture is an 'offer' – the viewer is constructed as an invisible onlooker. The characters are of the same height and on the same level. The angle is frontal, the two figures are at eye level. The full-length depiction of the males makes it a long shot that suggest an 'impersonal' relationship between the viewer and the represented participants. The frontal angle is the angle of maximal involvement and orientated towards action, showing the narrative for what it is – the distillation into conflict between two men.

## Lungile's use of the visual mode

The above analysis shows that Lungile uses the resources of the visual mode in a different way from how she uses performance and writing. The affordances of the visual mode are display and narrative. She has used display extensively in her meticulous, elaborate visual depictions of the different physical and material appearances of her two main characters. Such attention to the details of their appearances did not feature in her narrative performance, nor in her written account. It seems that for her, the visual mode offers her an opportunity to explore dimensions of her characters which she cannot explore in language: is this because she does not want to? Or because she does not have the linguistic resources to do so? Or because they cannot be readily explored in language in the same way? Take for example, the central tension in the drawing between two forms of male power. In her performance, she depicts this tension through the use of language and performative gestures which illustrate the differences in stature between two men. It is up to the viewer to imagine what these men look like. However, it is only when the viewer sees her images of the two men, drawn in careful detail, that it is possible to grasp fully their class, age and stylistic differences. The image is a complex sign of these cultural, social and symbolic differences. Her visual depiction fixes the images of these characters in a particular spatial and sensorial way, which provides a new context for their representation. Thus the use of the image produces distinctly different views or perspectives on the characters from those depicted in her performance and writing.

In the example of Lungile, it seems clear that in the moves across different modes, she is interacting differently with her narrative and reshaping aspects of the narrative according to how she wants 'the text to be taken'. In the visual mode, she has engaged in a meticulous and conscious way with what it means to 'see' their physical presence and their adornments. That is her interest: to deliberately and systematically focus on the entity 'character', to fix or stabilise the image of them in the viewer's mind, and to direct their attention to what seems to her to be the key theme in the narrative: the violent struggle between two very different *looking* male characters.

## Conclusion

In this chapter I have used a multimodal lens to throw light on the meaning-making practices of one student. This case study reveals a number of issues in relation to modes and representation. First, Lungile's use of her body compels us to reflect on the role of the body in modes. The study of her body in writing reveals the extent to which the full performing body disappears in the act of writing. Even though the act of writing still involves a sensory relation to light, space, the visual, the use of the hand and eye, the experience of writing is a process of dis-embodiment in which the speaking/gesturing body is stilled and silenced. The same may be said for her drawing. What this makes evident is how meaning-making in different modes occurs through/in the body and that multimodal performance uses the body in more visible ways than others.

How the body is used by individuals in acts of representation – in this case, performing, talking and writing – has its origins in culture and history of the practices. This study demonstrates how the cultural resources she draws on have particular histories and domains of provenance. She has an emotional relationship to each mode produced by these histories: modes carry memory, history and affect. In her use of body movements, sound and language in her performances, she draws on traces of memory of these performances, on the 'deep knowledge' she has acquired of these practices. It appears that her relationship to performance has an emotional link to her home, to her out-of-school experiences, and her relationship to writing is intimately linked to her experience of schooling. These sets of relations to modes affect learners' dispositions towards and productivity in different modes. It can also affect transformation from one mode into another: for example, from speech to writing, which in Lungile's case, appears to involve a loss of audience as well as a loss of the extended use of her body.

Different modes produce different 'takes' on the same subject or topic. Her interest in what is to be represented shifts as she moves in and out of, and across different modes. This is as much a result of what each mode has to offer, as it is a representation of her interested action. The performance, written and visual texts on Madevu Mbopha produce different perspectives and points of salience on the narrative. The performance mode offers the use of the body in its focus on display, narrative and enactment. Lungile's use of body elements vividly and explicitly conveys the immediacy of the narrative and the characters in real time. The written mode offers the use of action and narrative. In the written mode she narrows her focus to concentrate on making explicit the action, what happens to each of them. The visual mode offers the use of display and narrative. In her drawing, she depicts a moment of action, but far more detail has gone into the visual stylisation of each character in ways which are not present in any of her other texts.

From a pedagogical perspective, this case study offers much food for thought. Reading Lungile's texts as signs of learning reveals the processes of her creativity at work in quite explicit ways. Sadly, this creativity is often ignored or goes unrecognised in classrooms spaces, leading to comments such as, 'These children have no creativity'. The dominant view of creativity as a 'special talent' which only certain people possess is challenged by this perspective, which asserts that innovation and creativity is a normal condition of all human meaning-making (Kress *et al.* 2001). Such a perspective on creativity enables teachers to see their students' textual products and processes in a new light and can influence curriculum, pedagogy and assessment practices.

If, as I claim, Lungile inhabits different modes differently, and produces different 'takes' on the same subject through different modes, this has important implications for the structuring of teaching and learning. From this analysis, it appears that Lungile has preferred semiotic modes of representation. Although I have focused on only one student in this case study, I am willing to suggest that *all students* have preferred ways of knowing and representing, which usually remain unacknowledged and invisible in pedagogic settings. This has as much to do with the nature of pedagogic discourse and the narrow requirements of schooling, as it has to do with how teachers and learners collaborate to reproduce a dominant 'idea' of what schooling is and what it does. In mainstream classrooms, writing is the preferred and dominant mode for evaluating whether students pass or fail. What this case study shows is the richness of Lungile's performance texts and her drawing. In her school, Lungile would be evaluated on her *written text only*, which would constitute the formal assessment of her understanding, creativity, competence and engagement with her subject. This is highly problematic. The point I am trying to make is that *together*, these texts constitute an enormously interesting body of work from this one student.

Their interest is their multimodality: each text throws a different perspective on the Madevu Mbopha narrative. What this points to is the need for pedagogy to value different aspects of texts and to open up the space for students to produce multiple perspectives on the same subject. Working creatively with different modes and languages is one way to do this. This can be accomplished through the careful designing of classroom tasks and a conscious attention to engaging with students' diverse semiotic resources. I shall return to a fuller discussion of these issues in Chapter 6.

Different modes and languages of communication are privileged and maintained within different domains of power. In this case study, multimodal performance in an African language is privileged in the home of Lungile and written language in English is valued in the school. There is a different set of values attached to narrative styles in Lungile's home and in her school. These differences of value affect how students learn. They also have lasting influences on how students navigate their senses of identity and difference within these different sites.

This case study points to the need to consider ways of enabling students to get better at multimodality. In *More than Words: Multimodal Texts in the Classroom* (UKLA/QCA 2004) researchers ask: What does it mean to get better at multimodal representation? Their investigations showed that children need to be assisted to make appropriate choices to suit their communicative purposes. Teachers and learners need to focus on potentials of different modes and work at which mode is best suited to express particular meanings, asking the question: for this message, what can best be expressed in words and what in images? Examples of children's texts show how multimodality can provide different kinds of evidence of learning across a range of curriculum areas, and how images can express certain meanings that words cannot. The fact that Lungile performs the most successfully in the performance mode at this moment does not exclude her from inhabiting other modes with more ease, for example, writing. How she engages with different modes is not static but heavily dependent on the forms of mediation she is exposed to in her literacy classes. Structured mediation and scaffolding can help Lungile to improve her writing. Talking her through all her texts on Madevu Mbopha could help her to flesh out her writing and make it more interesting. For example, a productive discussion could be had between her and her teacher which focuses on 'translation' – how she could use metaphors, lexis and syntax to describe some of the finer detail of character which she depicts in her visual texts, for example, the differences in class and stature/height, weight, dress and bodily appearance. She could also refine her performance and drawing abilities through pedagogical processes which take forward her existing knowledge.

Chapter 4

# Drawing the unsayable

## The limits of language

### Introduction

The title of this chapter, *Drawing the unsayable*, points to the limits of language in expressing the arc of human experience, particularly experiences of fear, violation, pain and loss. The discursive and rational cannot account for all experience. The title also alludes to contexts where language and discourses are heavily policed, for example, where male discourse is dominant and women's voices are erased. In these situations, language practices become circumscribed by the dominant group. Resistance can come through various means, for example, contesting language practices, but in some contexts, resisting domination can lead to more violation. Locating meaning-making in forms of representation that go beyond language can become another form of resistance.

Multimodal analysis has sometimes been criticised for not making sufficient connections between the specificity of the micro studies and the macro 'big picture'. Jewitt points out:

> To realize the full potential of multimodality, research needs to make links between *what* is happening in the classroom and *why* it is happening – to ask how the micro social interactions of the classroom inflect, reflect and connect with the concerns of macro educational and broader social policies.
>
> (Jewitt 2008: 5)

In this chapter, I try to show how, at the micro level, children's choices of subject matter and the forms through which they choose to represent their meanings are revelatory of much broader social struggles in South Africa. I explore the limits of language through the writings and drawings of two girls and one boy, all of whom produced narratives on the subject of cannibals. A multimodal analysis of these children's multi-semiotic texts focuses on the question of modal choice: it is clear that the children make choices, whether consciously or unconsciously, to use different modes for different expressive purposes. These choices are not arbitrary but motivated. In the examples I present below, I argue that they are motivated by the constraints around what is considered 'unthinkable' and 'unsayable' within the context of what appears as naturalised cultural and social norms. These findings have important implications for pedagogy within contexts of diversity.

The area I address is one marked culturally in South Africa by silence: namely, adolescent sexuality. This includes sexual desire, sexual experience and sexual practices. Particularly for young girls, who are subject to high levels of sexual assault and violation from boys and older men, language fails them. Language is dangerous: talking about rape and sexual assault can lead to further violation. I suggest that in areas of experience culturally demarcated by silence, other semiotic modes offer possibilities for exploration of experience and feeling that language cannot. In the case study that follows, it is predominantly the visual mode that presents possibilities for the exploration of power, ambivalence and dread in relation to emerging masculinities and femininities.

The texts focused on in this chapter consist of pieces of writing and drawings by three children, all of whom participated in the Spruitview Storytelling Project described in Chapter 1. I chose to focus on these texts because significantly, 20 per cent of the stories children told in this project concerned cannibal or cannibal-like figures. These stories were written in local African languages and translated into English by the writers, except in the case of Zantotoza, where the translator was not the same as the writer.

The texts under discussion consist of a story and a drawing on 'Zantotoza' (Fig. 4.1); 'The Story of Apole' and the drawing of Apole (Fig. 4.2); the story 'The Monster Who Ate People' (Fig. 4.3) and the drawing (Fig. 4.4).

## The cannibal figure in South Africa

The cannibal or Zim figure has a rich archive of meaning in Southern African studies. In traditional African folkloric tales, the image of the cannibal is associated with the worst kinds of depravity, social disintegration and evil. Cannibals disrupt the natural social order, bringing anarchy and destruction. Cannibal characters are traditionally depicted as male (although there are occasionally female Zims), 'all mouth' swallowing monsters, with an insatiable desire for human flesh. As Scheub (1975) explains in his analysis of the Xhosa *ntsomi* tradition, the use of the Zim and cannibal characters throughout these texts produces a coherent overview of how Xhosa and Zulu societies construct the nature of evil. Certain episodes in these tales are structured around dangerous situations, which usually involve humans in confrontation with the forces of evil in the shape of a cannibal or Zim. For example, lost children will see a light in the distance and when they arrive at the homestead, a cannibal welcomes them. Cannibals assume different shapes and disguises as they migrate from tale to tale: they can be puffs of smoke, clouds of dust, beehives, fires in the dark, snakes and baboons. Audiences who are familiar with the *ntsomi* tradition recognise these disguises as signifiers of Zim-like qualities of evil and depravity. What is significant about the representation of these figures is that they emerge from contexts that are familiar and known. They are not situated in other worlds but part of the human world. This occurs through their connection to humanness: cannibals are creatures who have lost their humanity through eating humans:

> The Zim is the fallen angel of the *ntsomi* tradition. Indeed it is the likeness of man at his most vicious, but there is always an echo of an original perfection in the Zim's longing to re-enter the human world according to human standards.
>
> (Scheub 1975:77)

Examples of well-known Xhosa *iintsomi* which involve cannibals and Zim creatures are: 'A woman grows a claw and becomes a Zim'; 'A man puts a girl in a bag'; 'Two girls encounter a murderer'; 'Tselane, a boy murders his sister'; 'A surviving sister is victimised by a mbulu makhasana' (Scheub 1975). In all of these stories, the corruption brought to the natural social order through the presence of these creatures is profoundly destructive and dangerous. Adults challenge it and children attempt to outwit or destroy these creatures, sometimes successfully and sometimes not.

In Coplan's (1994) study of the word music of South Africa's Basotho migrants, *In the Time of Cannibals*, he analyses the genres of sung oral poetry performed by Basotho migrants who leave Lesotho to go and work on the South African goldmines. The image of cannibals is powerful in Basotho historical consciousness and is associated with the beginnings of the Basotho kingdom in the late 1820s when rival chiefs devoured their enemies on their paths to victory. The most notorious image of the cannibal was the king Shaka Zulu, who is said to have devoured chiefs and their clans who blocked his path, then forced them to eat one another. Thomas Mofolo, in his novel *Chaka*, finished in 1909, writes of the destruction wrought by Shaka and his followers in their cannibalistic rampages:

> It was at that time, that, on account of hunger, people began to eat each other as one eats the flesh of a slaughtered animal . . . And then after a few years the persecutions and sufferings from the east climbed over the Maloti mountains and entered Lesotho, and there too cannibals came into being because of hunger. This is the worst of all the evil things of those days, and that too arose because of Chaka, originator-of-all-things-evil.
>
> (Mofolo 1981:137)

Coplan traces the use of the cannibal image in Basotho migrant songs where it is used to refer to 'that cannibal of cannibals, white South Africa,' in the way it devours the Basotho people, lives off their labour and forces them to work in the bowels of the earth. In the mines, 'cannibal' (*lelimo*) acts as a metaphor for the devouring earth, and for the exploitative black 'boss boys' and their white counterparts, who ruthlessly extract their pound of flesh from black workers in their pursuit of higher pay. Thus the archetype of the cannibal is appropriated in diverse contexts as an 'unsavoury emblem of social pathology, parasitism, and disintegration in Sesotho', (Coplan 1994: 3).

There are many possible readings of the texts under discussion. As I have pointed out, the figure of the cannibal has a rich and complex archive in the literature and consciousness of Southern African people, and has been used in numerous ways to invoke forces of harm, violence and social disintegration. The interpretations I offer are suggestive and contingent: they offer a highly specific 'take' in order to reveal how children engage with and navigate the relationship between culture, gender and representation within their social worlds. The interpretations are situated against the macro backdrop of sexual violence in South Africa, in which the prevalence of male sexuality and violence against girl children and women is a massive social problem, threatening the very fabric of society in its ramifications for the uncontrollable spread of HIV/AIDS. South Africa has the sixth highest rates of HIV infection in the world (18.8 per cent of the population is infected) and considered to have the most severe form of the epidemic. For a number of reasons (gender inequalities and violence, physiological factors compounded by poverty) women face a greater risk of HIV infection than men: on average there are three women infected for every two men infected and the difference is greatest in the 15–24 age group where three young women are infected for every one man (Jewkes 2001; Collins and Stadler 2001; Johnson and Budlender 2002; Delius and Walker 2002; Delius and Glaser 2002; AIDS Foundation South Africa 2005 www.aids.org.za/hiv.htm).

The following analysis makes reference to certain styles or conventions of visual images in African art and popular culture. It is possible that students have drawn on these styles or conventions as resources to reflect their interests. In the same way that language can be considered immanent, continually in a process of being created rather than a fixed representation of reality, so material objects, images and conventions do not have fixed or stable meanings. Different styles and conventions are semiotic resources which are being constantly drawn upon in shifting contexts of use, shaped by community, culture and history.

In this analysis, I have worked with 'the actual' rather than the 'possible' in the interpretation of the students' drawings and writing, treating each text as a 'full semiotic object' which realises each child's interests in the particular historical moment in which the communication is taking place. It needs to be borne in mind, however, that each sign can never be more than a partial representation of the object, as the sign-maker's interest is always partial in the moment of making (Kress *et al.* 2001).

The analysis focuses on the following dimensions of the 'cannibal' texts:

- the use of representational resources, modes and aesthetic conventions;
- the visual representations of the boy, girl and cannibal;
- the verbal representation of the boy, girl and cannibal in the written stories;
- the thematic content in the written and visual texts;
- the interested action of the sign-makers;
- the relations between the micro analysis of texts and macro social processes.

## The written stories

### *'Zantotoza'*

The story of Zantotoza (Fig. 4.1) tells of a boy and his favourite beast, Zantotoza, who together, outwit cannibals whom they encounter in the forest. The cannibals instruct the boy to 'surrender' Zantatoza to them and if he refuses, they threaten to eat him. Zantotoza proves to be very resistant to being taken by the cannibals. He refuses 'to be skinned' until they instruct the boy to 'tell this beast to let himself be skinned', at which point the beast submits to his fate and dies. However, his defiance continues after his death: his meat 'refuses to be cooked' and the boy is threatened again to instruct him to 'let himself be cooked'. After the beast has been consumed, the boy asks them for his bones and skin. Using a knobkerrie as a magic wand, he instructs the skin and bones to wake up. Zantotoza is reconstituted as a living beast and together, they flee their captors. En route they come across another obstacle – the swollen river. The magical words are spoken once again, and the boy and his beast triumphantly cross the impassable river, to return home in one piece. On their arrival home, the story of their adventures and escape from the cannibal is related to the whole community.

The story is interesting at a number of levels. First, it works reflexively as a story about the art of storytelling itself, the artifice of fiction. When the boy and his beast arrive home, what they do is to 'tell everyone the story of what happened to them'. The readers of the Zantotoza story glean from this that stories are invented from extraordinary adventures that happen to people. They learn that storytelling is a communal experience, a forum in which everyday encounters, of the unexpected and extraordinary kind, can be talked about, enacted and shared. Stories are cultural bearers of meaning.

The plot consists of a situation of conflict in which the social order is disrupted by the forces of evil (the cannibals), and resolved through the combined efforts of good through nature (in the form of Zantotoza) and the child (in the form of the boy). Together, they triumph over social disintegration and restore the natural order. Through the encounter with the dangers presented by the cannibals, the boy and his animal are confronted with a

ZANTOTOZA

Once upon a time there lived a boy and his beast, Zantotoza. This Zantotoza was a favourite beast among all the beasts of that place in that household.

One day the boy and his beast, Zantotoza, went to the forest. They encountered cannibals. One said, 'Boy, surrender your beast to us. If you refuse, we shall eat you.'Then the cannibal took a rope and tied it around the beast's horns. When he pulled the rope, the beast just stood still. It did not enter the cannibal's gate. Then the cannibal said, 'Boy, tell this beast of yours to enter.' The boy said, 'Go in Zantotoza,' and the beast entered. They tried to skin it. That proved impossible as well. 'Hey boy, tell this beast to let himself be skinned!' 'Zantotoza, let yourself be skinned,' and the beast did so and he died.

They got all the meat into the pot. But the meat did not cook properly. 'Hey boy, tell this beast of yours to let himself be cooked!' The boy said, 'Be cooked, Zantotoza!' Then the meat became well cooked. The boy then told the cannibal to put the bones and the skin together after the meal. Having finished eating, the cannibals put the bones and the skin together.

The boy took the knobkerrie and said, 'Wake up, Zantotoza.' Zantotoza woke up and they quickly ran away from all the cannibals. The cannibals saw them. The honeymoon feasting was over in a flash. They instantly became hungry and chased them. The boy and the beast ran away. They reached a swollen river. The boy spoke, 'Cross the river, Zantotosa.' The cannibals cried because they had lost their meat.

The boy and the beast reached home that night and on their arrival they told everyone the story of what had happened to them.

*Figure 4.1 Zantotoza*: typed written text and drawing

supreme test of their bravery, cunning, bonding and prowess. Through various forms of trickery and disguise, the two outwit their enemies. The act of successfully passing through this metaphoric rite of passage (by death and drowning) with his animal by his side, initiates the boy into a state of heroic manhood in which 'the child and Nature and Society are one' (Scheub 1975: 85).

## *'The Story of Apole'*

In 'The Story of Apole' (Fig. 4.2), a mother barters with a cannibal, offering her unsuspecting daughter for his devouring instead of herself. In another form of a trickster tale, this time with girls as the protagonists, Apole and her friend outwit the cannibal (and the mother) by mirroring one another in their dress and putting scarification marks on their heads. The cannibal asks, 'Who is Apole?' and they reply as one, 'Me, me'. The cannibal cannot identify or 'see' the one girl from the other and is defeated by their trickery and disguises. In this story of betrayal and sacrifice, it is the children who are left by the adults to face a terrible fate and have to take action to save themselves. The heroes are the girl children who use cunning and an understanding of the power of physical beauty (the use of the 'red dress' and 'one line on the head') rather than physical strength, to confuse the predator and escape his clutches. The story uses archetypal symbols of desire and womanhood in the use of the 'red dress' (symbol of blood, menstruation, desire, sex, love and violence) and 'one line on the head' (identity marker for ethnic, gender, racial or aesthetic purposes) and 'Apole', a play on the word 'apple', with all its connotations of Eve and the forbidden fruit, ripeness, beauty, sensuality and womanhood.

## *'The Monster Who Ate People'*

The third story, 'The Monster Who Ate People' (Fig. 4.3), is the tragic story of the young girl who did not get away. In this story, the girl child is left by her mother who leaves her family home in the small village to go and live in town. Tselane elects to stay in the village with her 'cat' and 'her friend'. When her mother brings her food, unbeknown to them, the monster that ate people is watching them. Like the wolf in the folktale, 'The Wolf and the Seven Kids', this monster disguises himself as her mother, and tries to trick her into opening the door. She sees through his disguise but he seeks the help of a witch to change his voice. This time, Tselane falls for his ploy. She is devoured by the monster and 'that was the end of Tselane'.

In this tale, it is interesting to compare the isolation and 'alone-ness' of the child with the supportive relationships described in the two previous stories. Through her choice to remain loyal to her father, and not follow her mother to town, she finds herself without protection. Like Apole and the boy in Zantotoza, Tselane comes to understand that she is in mortal danger but she seems unable to summon any help (in the form of nature or humans) or save herself through her own resources. The bleakness of her situation is signalled by the absence of community and a mother who has abandoned her, leaving her food outside the door as though she is some kind of animal. In this tale, unlike in 'Zantotoza', magic is used to destroy the girl rather

# THE STORY OF APOLE

One day there was a girl who lived with her mother. Her mother liked tc go to the bushes to fetch wood. One day Apole's mother saw a cannibal. And the cannibal said, 'I will eat you.' Apole's mothar said, 'Don't eat me, I will give you my baby.' And the cannibal said, 'How will I see her?' Apole's mother said, 'You will see her in a red dress.'

Apole dressed in a red dress, she went to her friend and her friend said, 'You look beautiful.' And her friend put on the red dress and they went out to play. They saw a cannibal. He asked, 'Who is Apole?' And the girls both said, 'Me, me!' And the cannibal was very angry. He went back to the bushes.

Apole's mother went to the bushes. She saw the cannibal. She said, 'Did you find her?' The cannibal said, 'No, I will eat you.' And Apole's mother said, 'Don't eat me, I will give you my baby.' And the cannibal said, 'How will I see her?' Apole's mother said, 'She has one line on her head.' And she went back home and said, 'Apole, let me cut one line on your head.' And Apole said, 'Okay.'

She then went to her friend. Her friend said, 'You look beautiful!' And she asked her if she could also cut a line on her head and Apole agreed. She cut her friend's head. They both went out to play. They saw the cannibal and he said, 'Who is Apole?' They both said, 'Me, me!' and the cannibal was very angry.

At last Apole was saved.

*Figure 4.2 The Story of Apole*: typed written text and drawing

THE MONSTER WHO ATE PEOPLE

Once upon a time there was a little girl called Tselane. She and her mother lived in a small village. One day Tselane's mother decided to go and buy a house in town. Tselane refused to go, saying that she wanted to stay in her father's house. She liked staying in the village with her friends and relatives.

Tselane's mother went to stay in town. Tselane stayed in the village with her cat and her friend. One day Tselane's mother came and called her from outside saying, 'Tselane, Tselane, come and get your food.' Tselane replied,'I'm coming mother.' She went outside to get her food. She waved goodbye to her mother and went back inside.

The monster who ate people was listening to them. He went home to get some food, then went back to Tselane's house. He called out, 'Tselane, Tselane,' in a terrible voice. Tselane was afraid to reply. She said, 'I won't get out of here, I know you monster, you want to eat me, go away!'

The monster went to see a witch to change his voice. He came back next morning and his voice sounded like Tselane's mother's voice. He called for Tselane and she went outside to get her food, thinking it was her mother. Then the monster grabbed her and ate her up. When her mother came she did not find her and started crying. She asked everyone what had happened and they told her the whole story.

And that was the end of Tselane.

*Figure 4.3 The Monster Who Ate People*: typed written text

than to enable her survival. The story seems to suggest that staying loyal to fathers or, more specifically, choosing to live with fathers rather than mothers, is a road that leads to disaster.

## The drawings of cannibals

Each child has drawn his or her cannibal figure differently. Viewing these figures from a comparative perspective throws interesting light on the absences and presences in each representation. It also indicates what each child has chosen as criterial to 'cannibalness'; in this sense, each visual text can be thought of as an identity text which carries the traces of its author within.

*Figure 4.4 The Monster Who Ate People*: drawing

### ***Drawing: 'Zantotoza'*** (see Figure 4.1)

This cannibal figure is drawn as a male human figure, with a bulbous human face, a moustache, and tufts of hair. He is the same size as the other human figure in the drawing, who has been given the name Steven, the same name as the author of the story. The cannibal is naked – which is contrasted with the other male figure of Steven, who is clothed. The cannibal figure has an assegai in his left hand, which he is pointing and waving at the Steven figure and the cow, who are positioned to the right, in front of him. His left leg is suspended in the air, suggesting a running movement. He is drawn in profile.

### ***Drawing: 'The Story of Apole'*** (see Figure 4.2)

The cannibal is a male human figure, slightly larger in size than Apole, the half-human, half-apple female figure in the drawing. The cannibal resembles a young man, with a sharply pointed nose, pointed chin, protruding ears, two eyes and eyebrows, one pupil of the eye more emphasised than the other, which seems to be glaring simultaneously at the figure of Apole and at the viewer. He has a crescent shaped mouth full of carefully drawn sharp teeth, a distinguishing marker of identity. His right arm is fatter than the left arm, and his right hand has fatter fingers than the left hand. He is wearing a pair of knee-length shorts, and a belt or a button at the top of the shorts. He has thin legs and small knobs on his knees. He is wearing some kind of footwear, perhaps sandals. As he looks at Apole and the viewer, he is saying (in the speech bubble), 'I am a cannibal.'

### *Drawing: 'The Monster Who Ate People'* (see Figure 4.4)

In this drawing, the cannibal resembles a mutant, anthropomorphic creature that walks upright like a bear or a gorilla, in the style of a King Kong or Tarzan figure. It is at least twice the size of the female character in the story and in the drawing. It is drawn in profile, has a large eye in the middle of the side of its head, with a pupil which has been coloured in black. It has a little red snout, a mouth with teeth carefully drawn, and a long red tongue hanging out of its mouth. Drops of liquid are dripping off its tongue. The right foot of this cannibal is lifted, suggesting it is in motion. Its right paw, with three claw-like fingers, is touching or pushing down on the head of the little girl. At the same time it is lifting the girl off the ground with its right leg. The girl is immobilised, trapped between its foot and its paw. She is weeping and looking directly at the viewer.

In the case of Figure 4.1, the sign-maker seems to be drawing on style or conventions of black male figures depicted in Bushman/San rock art which are found all over Southern Africa dating from 2,000 to 4,000 years ago. The San were hunter-gatherers who roamed the countryside looking for game and food. The schematic drawing of the cannibal as a naked male hunting figure, delicately drawn in a state of motion, about to throw a spear or assegai is typical of how black males are represented in Bushman/San rock art. The drawing of the cow in Figure 4.1 is very similar in design to the traditional clay cows made by young boys in rural communities as objects of play. These clay cows have been made for hundreds of years and are still made by small boys in rural communities today.

In Figure 4.2, the cannibal is drawn as a contemporary young male, dressed in modern clothing – shorts and sandals. The markers of his status as cannibal, his 'otherness', seem to be fairly discrete: a mouth full of teeth, an enlarged pupil of his one eye and the little protruding knobs on his knees. It is interesting to note that these particular features – the enlarged eye, the teeth and the knobs on the knees – appear in traditional Tsonga carved figures of wood which are used in initiation ceremonies for men. Figures such as these are used in the instruction of initiates, as young men pass from boyhood into adulthood. The male carved figure is often used with a female figure to illustrate teachings about sexual and social mores.

In Figure 4.4, the cannibal is drawn as a larger than life, mythical animal creature in motion, with one large eye and a long protruding tongue similar in design to some of the modelled clay sculptures of animals, birds and anthropomorphic figures used in girl initiation ceremonies (Harber 1998). These figures were part of ritual ceremonies and the ceremonial sacrifice of animals. This figure also draws on images of King Kong and Tarzan, which abound in contemporary popular media and comic-book culture.

Each image of the cannibal figure is highly personal and individual, bearing the distinctiveness of its maker. At the same time each image is a hybrid text, composed from a range of sources and styles which speak simultaneously to a mythic idealised past and to modernity and the contemporary world of popular culture and media. These are rich cultural identity texts in which the makers are visually and discursively engaging with the idea of 'cannibal', in all its material and mythic manifestations.

## Drawings of the humans

A comparative perspective on how the human figures are represented produces interesting distinctions between them. In Figure 4.1, the cannibal is in profile and in action, but the figure of the boy, significantly also labelled Steven (Steven is the name of the boy who produced the text), is positioned between the cannibal and the cow. He is the protagonist in the centre of the action, the hero who is protecting his favourite beast from the cannibal-intruder. The whole drawing depicts a moment in action, an event which is taking place. This is distinct from the more static image of display in Figure 4.2 of Apole and the cannibal. In some sense, the image is working both as narrative and display. The scene is styled as a typical 'chase' scene from a picture or comic book, or movie, with the baddie running after the goodies, brandishing his stick in the air. The specificity of this image brings to mind countless photographic and television images of large, white South African boers chasing after or chasing off black people from their farms or homesteads for 'illegal squatting' – a kind of cultural stereotype of racism in apartheid South Africa. At the same time, it also has elements of a 'traditional' African male narrative of a herd boy looking after his cattle, protecting his favourite cow from marauders and thieves.

Steven depicts his relationship to the cannibal as heroic: the artist himself is the main actor in the drawing. It is also interesting that the cannibal is drawn without clothing, whilst the Steven-hero character wears his clothing as a marker of progress, civilisation, culture. The drawing can be read as the child's encounter with the Other as the primitive, defined by fear and revulsion. The cannibal is depicted as Other, the aggressor, the savage, the uncivilised. Steven both as actor in the image and child, is distancing himself from the forces that this cannibal creature represents – the 'primitive', the violent and chaotic – to show himself as the conquerer and repressor of the evil forces. He is the force of modernity – the contemporary boy hero in an adventure in which he is the central actor. Males act in the world. They have power: they rescue, save, fight off enemies and protect their herds (whether they be 'women' or 'cattle'). Steven's interest in his own emerging masculinity as a predatory male fighting off other predators in order to protect his property is inscribed in this image.

In Figure 4.2 of Apole and the cannibal, the image as a whole is working as display and acknowledgement of a state of being. The cannibal and Apole are in conflict but it is not a conflict of action, as in the drawing of Steven. The cannibal has considerable presence and agency: he is facing the viewer and interacting with Apole and the viewer through his presence, his gaze and his speech, in the speech bubble. By his side floats some kind of container – a bag in which to hide her? – as in the famous folktale tale about the Zim who kidnaps a young girl and hides her in his sack. The image is a good example of the image as classification (the 'I am x' relation) with some interaction introduced through speech bubbles. In their relationship to the viewer, the cannibal figure and Apole are arranged in symmetrical form across the space with a left-right structure, as though the artist is arranging a display of these objects for the viewer.

More scrutiny of the cannibal's gaze reveals layers of ambivalences. It is significant that the cannibal figure is looking at Apole out of one eye, and at the viewer out of the other. His gaze controls his object of desire and the outside eye of the viewer that witnesses this desire. Apole's gaze is directly at the viewer, one eye slightly enlarged. The power of the gaze in sexual courtship rituals is well documented, for example in the lyrics of a popular *isicathamiya* song, '*Uthando*' (Love), composed by Nkone Dlamuka of the Lion Singers from the Valley of a Thousand Hills in KwaZulu-Natal:

| | |
|---|---|
| *Ngaba iyamthanda-nje* | (Just because she loves him) |
| *Uma uyibheka* | (If he looks at her) |
| *Uyazibona izihlathi zigcwele Uthando* | (You can see her face shines with love) |
| *Uma ibona abakubo* | (If she looks at his family) |
| *Iyashalaza* | (She's shy) |
| *Ibheke phansi njengesambane* | (She glances down like the ant-eater) |
| *Uma ibona yena* | (If she sees him) |
| *Ivusa amehlo kancane* | (Her eyes widen a little) |
| *Ibisiyamamatheka* | (And then she smiles) |
| *Kodwa ngoba akanaluthonje* | (But because he's got nothing it doesn't mean a thing). |

(Gunner 2006: 89)

Research by Henderson on adolescent sexuality among boys and girls in New Crossroads township in the Western Cape reveals the extent to which the nature of the girl's gaze is regarded as a marker of respect or disrespect. A 17-year-old boy commented:

> When you look directly at a girl, the girl must look down. She mustn't look directly at you. This shows respect.
>
> (Henderson 1999: 18)

In the image of Apole, she does not look directly at the boy/cannibal: can this be read as a sign of 'respect'?

The drama between them unfolds with the opening lines: 'I am Apole' and 'I am a canibal [sic]'. The rest is to be imagined. The speech bubbles from which they proclaim their identities, their stances, their ontologies are a way to anchor the text. The image is composite, combining words and image. Like textbook illustrations, each subject/object needs to be labelled and classified. There is a consciousness in the artist of comic-book conventions, of the relationship between image and words. The narrative is caught in the tension between them.

The image of the girl figure, Apole, is a sign with multiple significations. It is a visual pun on popular images of woman as Eve, as objects of desire, 'apples' ready for eating. Apole is a mythic creature with the body of a young girl and a face that is both a human and non-human (an apple). A face that can be eaten. Significantly, in her written story, the child uses the name 'Apole' not *apple*, to refer to her main character. She makes no mention of the main character having a face that resembles an apple. In the move from the written text to the image, 'Apole' is translated or transformed into a visual pun.

The language of sex abounds with metaphors relating to eating. Sex is an act of consumption. In tsotsitaal, an urban township slang, girls are 'tjerries' (cherries) or 'wiebits' (wee bits). A white girl is 'hoendervleis' (chicken meat). To have sex is to 'eet' (eat) and to fancy someone is to 'smaak' them, slang for relishing food or drink. In an Umtata youth study (Wood and Jewkes 1998: 9), youth referred to sex as an inexorable physical need, such as 'tasting', 'chowing' (literally: eating) and girls are referred to as 'cherries'. The boys are those who eat, and the girls are eaten. Girls are referred to as 'tasty' and 'ripe' for plucking. As one girl from Umtata put it:

> Boys use us, they need sex, then after tasting you, they leave you for other girls.
>
> (Wood and Jewkes 1998: 8)

The power relations between Apole and the cannibal are intriguing. Compositionally, they are arranged side by side, as equals, standing upright facing the viewer. The way they stand resembles male and female wooden or clay figures used in puberty initiation ceremonies to teach about sexual practices and mores (Harber 1998). The fact that the cannibal figure has been represented as quite ordinary, dressed in the style of an average young man, is revelatory and distressing. He is a kind of 'dude' whose markers of danger and desire are almost rendered invisible. What the sign-maker seems to be saying is: *the cannibal is one of us*. Scheub has noted in his study of the cannibal figure:

> It is vital to a proper understanding of nature of the Zim to note its familiar surroundings, that it springs from a context that is known.
> (Scheub 1975: 79)

The cannibals among us are young men with sharp teeth and protruding eyeballs who desire to eat apples (young girls). But unlike the image of the girl trapped by the cannibal in Figure 4.4, Apole is depicted as separate, still free, although subject to his predatory eyes. Apole's separateness could express some contestation and ambivalence in relation to the male cannibal's claims to devour. She acknowledges her gendered construction as 'an apple for eating' but is holding on to her individual agency and power. It seems to me that the artist's interest is in negotiating her relationship to sexuality and desire (in the sense of both affirming and contesting) and this is motivating her choice of signifiers and their arrangement on the page.

Unlike Figure 4.1 of the boy as hero, escaping from the clutches of the cannibal, the depiction of the young girl in Figure 4.4 is an image of entrapment and surrender. There is little sense of the girl as agent with any power. We view a moment in action – the young girl weeping while the cannibal pins her down between his claws and paws. In terms of the sign-maker's relations to the cannibal, she represents it as an overpowering, large force, the protruding tongue a symbol of sexuality dripping drops of saliva, blood, semen, a force from which there is no escape. The presence of the tree in the lower third of the drawing, fixed between the girl and the monster, is covered in fruit, with the branch like a phallic object protruding from the main trunk. The symbolism resonates with the Apole fruit image in Figure 4.2. The drawing is full of phallic images – the shark-like 'branches' are coming out of fertile, fruity trees and fish are swimming through water. All that is to be done is for young girls to weep at their state of dread as male predators close in.

A postgraduate student from Eritrea associated Figure 4.4 with an Eritrean marriage practice known as 'abduction'. In this practice, a bridegroom is allowed to take any woman from the fields, to make her his wife and then send someone to her parents to inform them that their daughter has been abducted and to arrange a legal marriage. This practice occurs for different reasons:

> Sometimes they do it if the bride is found not to be a virgin or if the bride who is supposed to marry by her parents' arrangement 'gets lost' (hides) on the day of her marriage. Then the bridegroom, to save himself and his family from this shame, has a right to take any of her sisters

> or any mature lady from the streets by force. We see in the drawing that the doors and windows are closed; there is nobody who can save this lady whilst she is being taken by the animal (a different representation of a male human being). This implies that the act is accepted by the society and she cannot be protected from entering into this unwilling marriage. We can see that the sun is drawn as the only sympathetic observer from the entire environment. And because the sun is categorised in most cultures as a female, the sun is also unable to help this lady.
> (Abraham 2001)

## Signs: writing and drawing

This body of multimodal texts is intriguing at a number of levels. First, to understand them as complex signs, as 'texts' which inflect the micro and macro sites in which they are embedded. As such, this approach to text connects with Bakhtin's (1981) idea of the chronotrope, which is a unit of analysis and a way of reading texts as x-rays of the forces at work in the cultural system from which they spring. A focus on this body of texts can reveal the multifaceted forces at work in the cultural system in which they are constituted (Bhattacharya *et al.* 2007). Second, to understand them from a multimodal perspective in terms of how each child is using the semiotic potentials of writing and drawing to communicate. I shall deal with each issue in turn.

### *Texts as x-rays*

It seems obvious that this body of work on the subject of cannibals is tapping into prevailing concerns in private and public spheres around adolescent sexuality, gender and violence. Each sign-maker is representing a particular perspective on this idea through forms of narrative in different modes: a written story, on the one hand, and an image, on the other (with some language in two of the images). Each text is a metaphor. The concept of metaphor applies to image as well as to language. Metaphors create new ways of expressing ideas through the translation of one thing into another.

The cannibal figure in Southern African and African studies has a history. Cannibals are metaphors for forces of inchoate violence, depravity and evil. They are usually associated with males who use trickery and disguise to kidnap or trap children and/or adults into their domains. They crave young girls. In each of these texts, the cannibal figure is depicted as a threat to the lives of children. Each child reads her or himself into the story or drawing (the children depicted in the stories are of similar age to the authors/artists). In the girls' texts, the cannibal figure represents male sexual power and energy as a dominating, dangerous force. In the boy's texts, the cannibal is to be feared but conquered.

It seems plausible that the cannibal and its relations to the child figure/s in these texts can be read as a metaphor for masculinities and femininities surrounding adolescent sexual practices and mores. Research into the sexual practices of South African adolescent boys and girls has highlighted the alarming degrees of violence within youth sexual relationships in the forms of physical assault and forced sex (Wood *et al.* 1996; Centre for the Study of Violence and Reconciliation 1997; Wood and Jewkes 1998; Henderson 1999; Jewkes *et al.* 2002). Rape, coercion and violence are common features of adolescent sexual behaviour (loveLife, 2001: 1) and gender-based violence against girls is a matter of ongoing concern in schools (Haffejee 2006). Young women are subject to assault (ranging from slappings to beatings with objects and stabbing) and sexual coercion (on a spectrum from begging to gang rape) by partners and others. Figures on rape between April 2004 and March 2005 indicate that 55,114 cases were reported to the police.

In one report on Xhosa adolescents in Umtata (Wood and Jewkes 1998), the use of violence by boys was a way of imposing the 'rules' of the relationship which included 'rules' around girls' rejections of proposals of love, their attempts to end the relationship, their refusals of sex and their attempts to check up on boys' infidelity. It was found in this study that how to go about gaining and keeping girlfriends or boyfriends were overwhelming preoccupations of the youth, with their male and female identities substantially constructed in terms of success in sexual relationships. These emerging identities are played out in struggles for power and positions in the peer group, with high levels of vulnerability:

> With evaluations of self-worth and power so critically dependent on the actions of others, boys and girls remain inherently vulnerable. Thus boys used physical coercion against girls in order to maintain their fantasies of power. Girls were restricted in their ability to resist violent men for fear of losing a relationship of 'status' and, whilst characterising men as irresponsible and deceitful, were eager accomplices in acts of deceit against other women when these increased their power and position within the female peer group.
>
> (Wood and Jewkes 1998: 2–3)

In a nationwide study conducted in 2004 with 270,000 South African boys and girls between the ages of 10 and 19, it was found that the prevalence of sexual violence against children leads to attitudes that condone or expect such violence. Fifty per cent of the respondents felt that 'sexual violence does not include forcing sex with someone you know'. Thirty per cent said, 'Girls do not have a right to refuse sex with their boyfriend' and a total of 8.6 per cent of all respondents had been forced to have sex in the last year. In a survey conducted with adolescent girls in KwaZulu-Natal in 2001,

24 per cent of girls interviewed said they were 'forced' or 'tricked' into their first sexual experience (www.irinnews.info./S_report.asp; retrieved 16.02.07).

### *Shame and silence*

Issues of sexual violence have to be seen in relation to the cultural and social taboos which surround speaking out. A woman student responded to these images thus:

> I believe that language 'fails them' [young girls] because of their cultural backgrounds. In the culture where they come from, some things are not supposed to be called by names, especially when it comes to sexual matters . . . The reason being that if they have to repeat it to adults it means they have to mention every finer detail, which they cannot, because some things are not to be said in their culture. Some things are referred to as taboo from the culture they come from. I also had an experience where I was put in a 'mini-court' for expressing an unacceptable message to my husband's aunts. I was newly wed and still new in the family. We went to a family funeral where all the 'makotis' had to serve the in-laws. I took basins and put some warm water for the two aunts to go and wash themselves. I called them to go into one of the huts. They were sitting behind the yard or what we call 'lapa'. They said I must bring the water outside to them. I said but you are not going to have privacy. They replied and said I have insulted them. In other words, I meant if they wash outside they would not wash themselves properly and that they would not wash their private parts. The whole thing was misinterpreted as an insult. Therefore they concluded that I had insulted them. They called some old ladies to judge the case and my fine was that I should buy four litres of cold drink for them . . . In our culture you have to be very careful of what you say in the company of old people. Some things are not supposed to be said by young girls and women. This shows that women are oppressed in our culture.
>
> (Mohlala 2001: 2)

In a report on gender equity in education, Wolpe *et al.* (1997) comment on the taboos in relation to 'open' discussion of sexual violence, maintaining that there is a 'remarkable silence' around general acts of sexual harassment and violence which are perceived as a 'normal' part of 'growing up' or an example of 'boys being boys'. Henderson describes the silences surrounding boys' and girls' sexuality in New Crossroads in the Western Cape and how silences in relating sexual experience and desire take on differing inflections in relation to boys and girls:

> Although boys have a predatory language with which to express their pursuit of girls, girls are far less voluble concerning their relations to boys. A more general silence in communicating sexual matters between parents and their children marks respectful avoidance between generations.
> (Henderson 1999: 4)

Her work shows that this lack of communication of sexual matters needs to be placed in relation to increasing sexual violence towards young children and especially young girls.

The silences of young girls surrounding sexuality are the most powerful in relation to rape, where girls prefer to remain silent. Henderson (1999: 23) suggests that this silence in language comes about because speaking about this violation turns the girl into 'an object of curiosity and titillation'. Thus the amplification of her experience through speech 'amplifies her own sense of shame'. This sense of shame is endorsed in her peer group: her friends protect her through their presence and insist that 'her recovery will be affected through silence, through forgetfulness'.

Verbal language is dangerous and unsatisfying:

> The terms that we may apply to illuminate areas of silence too quickly take on the character of unsatisfying speech, speech that slips past what we attempt to explore or communicate. Yet it is just such areas of silence that circumscribe painful areas of social limitation for particular groupings of people and that need to be addressed by the social sciences.
> (Henderson 1999: 23)

Seremetakis (1994) has written that splits between the 'public' and the 'private', between the 'sayable' and the 'unsaid', create zones of 'inadmissible memory' that constitute a space for forgetfulness:

> The cultural construction of the 'public' and the sayable in turn creates zones of privatised, inadmissible memory and experience that operate as spaces of amnesia and anaesthesia. . . . As the zones of amnesia and the unsaid expand in tandem with the increasingly formulaic and selective reproduction of public memory, the issue of narrativity becomes a zone of increasing political and cultural tension.
> (Seremetakis 1994:19–20)

It seems to me that the children's texts are marked by such splits between the 'public' and 'sayable', and the 'private' and 'inadmissable'. An important split occurs in the translation across mode, in the shift from writing to drawing, from language to image. All three stories are written within the generic conventions of folkloric tales: they are stories which the children know well and have listened to many times. They are part of their cultural heritage. Each story has an established structure from which there are minor deviations. However, in the act of translation or transformation from the written story to the image, a distinct form of creativity appears: although both written narrative and image offer possibilities for the exploration of self, it is within the realm of the image that these children find a certain freedom from convention and taboo.

The written story and drawing of Zantotoza illustrate choices around the 'public' and the 'private', particularly in relation to ideas of masculinity. The 'public' text, owned by history and the 'oral community', is the written narrative. In the material and physical act of drawing, the abstract idea of 'the boy' who is the protagonist in the written text becomes an 'I', a signed self-portrait, in which the artist draws *himself* into the hero of the tale. The 'unsayable' or that which is 'concealed' in the written text becomes 'seen' in the visual text. Image offers the possibility to make visible a private self which the written text conceals. These relations to image and writing are historically and culturally located within larger communicative practices around 'the sayable' and 'the written word'. Thus, for example, writing is part of the domain of the 'public'; it is impersonal, distant and associated with official, public selves. To write means to follow certain accepted conventions whereas drawing offers more potential for exploration, for exploration of the imaginary world.

'The story of Apole' was written first in Zulu and translated by the author into English. In the same way that Steven in 'Zantotoza' uses different modes to represent the split between the public and the private self, the author of Apole produces an account of the Apole tale in her written text which follows established conventions around this genre. In the shift into drawing, she plays creatively and expressively with an image of the cannibal and the girl, giving a different shape and form to these characters. Her written text does not suggest that Apole is half-apple, half-girl; she is 'a girl who lived with her mother'. And the cannibal is not described in the written text as a young man with sharp teeth and pointed features, with knobs on his knees. He is simply 'the cannibal'. But the visual text offers the writer the possibilities of re-presenting 'the inadmissible', that which cannot be spoken – that the cannibal, like the child abuser or rapist, walks by our side. He is our neighbour, he is one of us. Furthermore, the cannibal can show his face. But the girl Apole, like the young girls in Crossroads, hides behind her apple face, wearing her mask of 'inadmissible' silence to protect her from further violation and shame.

## Concluding remarks

In 1995, Kress described the subject English as a number of curricula around which the English teacher has to 'construct some plausible principles of coherence'. It is a curriculum of communication via its teaching of English as language. It is a curriculum of culture and sociality, carried through, for example, the choices and values of texts and pedagogies around texts. And it is also the subject in which questions of ethics and morality are explored:

> . . . English is the subject in which ethics, questions of social, public morality are constantly at issue . . . in terms of giving children the means of dealing with ethical, moral issues . . . and absorbing the ethos developed in the classroom.
>
> (Kress 1995: 5–6)

This chapter raises deep and troubling questions for English teachers (and language teachers in general) about the boundaries of responsibility and ethics in relation to areas of social crisis which affect their students. If a central aim of English teaching is to encourage students to 'represent' who they are, what they feel and know, in an open, creative and respectful environment, then it seems important for teachers to acknowledge the *dialogic* nature of the students' signs. In other words, the setting up of tasks which ask for openness and personal exploration from students needs to be seen as an invitation for dialogue, for negotiation. When speaking, writing or making visual texts, the student as speaker/writer anticipates the potential response of the addressee. Each student is thus an active subject producing different signs which are addressed to different readers/viewers although, in the main, the addressee in the classroom is the teacher. If students' signs are dialogic, then how should teachers respond, particularly in highly controversial areas surrounded by silence, stigma and taboo? I present a number of positions on this below.

## Language and silence

Suffering, like pain, exists beyond language. Who has the right to speak? Who has the right to silence? As Das (1996) notes, what is the place of the relation between pain and culture that a culture has evolved? In language and literacy classrooms where talk and words are the focus of study and the privileged means through which communication is achieved, an unproblematic relation exists between talk and what is understood as 'authentic communication'. Articulateness, volubility, and general eagerness to talk are perceived as positive and desirable qualities in learners (Jaworksi and Sachdev 1998). Silence and reticence are considered detrimental to learning. It may be that there is place for silence – an inclusive silence which allows for positivity and presence of being, rather than absence. This silence acknowledges that there are things which are unspeakable, which cannot be said. This kind of silence acknowledges human beings' rights to silence in the context of power exercised by teachers in placing students under obligation to speak.

In this sense, students can be offered a choice of silence, in the same vein as a choice to speak. What is being suggested is an ethics of pedagogy in relation to children's rights to dignity and choice concerning how they wish to communicate their meanings in classrooms spaces.

## Signs and 'transitional spaces'

In an article on violence and masculinities in the domestic sphere of family life and interpersonal relations in post-apartheid South Africa, Sideris (2004) discusses how a fourteen year old abused boy makes use of his diary as a 'transitional space' for exploring the self within his social and political world. Winnicott (1958) talks about the 'transitional space' as a space of 'rest', a 'relief' from the tension of separating and connecting inner and outer reality. It is a space in which paradoxes – inner and outer, self and other, individual desires and shared realities – are juggled and negotiated, a space of personal creativity which provides a site for 'questioning and challenging, for renegotiating those meanings and values given by external reality'. In the case of the diary of Borsh Maziba, he draws on symbols and discourses in his social world to try to make meaning of the domestic violence in his family. He selects entries from his school books, stories of maternal care and the experiences of Nelson Mandela as a source of inspiration, to give expression to his hope and pain. Sideris shows how through the activity of writing something between a monologue and dialogue, Borsh Maziba is able to represent his emotions and thoughts to a reader. As the diary progresses, he becomes more reflective and philosophical, relating his experiences of personal violation to issues of freedom and his rights. Sideris suggests that dialogue in the 'transitional space' can provide a potential arena for dismantling previous ways of thinking and feeling and for making connections between the personal and wider social forces. However there is anxiety released in this process which must be supported by reliable and caring relationships (Sideris 2004: 26).

What this example does seem to suggest is that representing one's inner and outer worlds can be a powerful way of challenging the normative and conceptualizing alternative realities. This is a strong argument for thinking about English classrooms as contexts in which 'transitional spaces' can be created for students to explore and negotiate their personal and broader social worlds. However, the anxiety that this produces needs to be supported by school counselling services or other kinds of support structures which can help students to navigate the difficulties and challenges of their everyday lives. Unfortunately, in many schools in South Africa, there simply aren't such services available and the responsibility of supporting and guiding students becomes the task of the English and/or Guidance teachers.

This chapter demonstrates some of the possibilities and forms that this 'transitional space' can take. How such 'spaces' occur will vary from classroom to classroom and can be jointly negotiated with students in relation to their linguistic, cultural and epistemological diversity. Whilst Borsh Maziba chose to use a diary format as his space of 'rest' and personal creativity, the children in this chapter chose to work with the modes of writing and drawing in ways which negotiated some of the paradoxes of their everyday realities. The meanings of their signs lie in the relation between the visible and the concealed. It is conceivable that in the cannibal texts, the students are using writing to express a more 'public' self and drawing to express a more 'private' concealed self. In negotiating sexuality, desire, power and taboo, image here seems to offer more space for ambiguity. There is a sense that students are expressing relations of distance and respect with regard to writing, an implicit belief that writing does not admit the private, individual 'I' but records and documents public statements. Students' beliefs about what writing is and what it does, what the visual is and what it does, are related to their histories of how semiotic resources are used and transformed within the worlds they inhabit and move through in their everyday lives. In the case of the image of Apole and the cannibal 'boy' figure, the invisible is contained within the visible: that which is concealed is that which can be seen.

This chapter has explored the limits of language in the representation of feeling, desire and pain. I have suggested that choice of mode may not always be an issue of affordances, a case of whether one mode, technically or formally, is 'better' for meaning-making than another. 'Better' may involve a social or political dimension in the sense that it may be in one's better interests to choose another way to say something. Or that it simply may not be possible to say something for reasons of stigma or taboo. In areas of dread, ambivalence, terror and pain, people can be silent, often seeking beyond language to express what they know and how they feel.

Chapter 5

# 'Fresh Stories'

## Multimodality and points of fixing in the semiotic chain

### Introduction

The focus of this chapter is on an early literacy project in multimodality and narrative, the Olifantsvlei 'Fresh Stories' Project, which was carried out during 2001 with Grade 1 and 2 teachers and children at a primary school in Eikenhof, south of Johannesburg. The aim of the Olifantsvlei 'Fresh Stories' Project was to develop a body of imaginative, local, 'fresh stories' based on and arising from the children's lives and local experiences. Within the broader political frame, this interest in local stories is linked to post-apartheid identity quests and various 'dramas of self-definition' in which South Africans are engaged (Jacobs 1992).

The Olifantsvlei 'Fresh Stories' Project was a conscious attempt to work with multimodality, creativity and pedagogy with young children, in order to build on and extend children's existing semiotic resources and local knowledges. The use of multimodal pedagogies in working through the Olifantsvlei project led to the production of multiple semiotic objects in different sequenced stages and in different modes: 2D drawings, writing, 3D figures, spoken dialogues and multimodal play performances. The production of these textual objects was in response to a central concept which ran through the project, namely, the creation of a body of characters which would form the basis of storytelling, play-making and writing. These multimodal textual objects have been described by Kress (Jewitt and Kress 2003) as points of 'fixing' in the chain of semiosis. The focus of this chapter is on the 3D doll/child figures produced by the children. In relation to the semiotic chain, they illuminate a number of important issues concerning multimodality, materiality, creativity and aesthetics within different contexts of meaning-making. Through the particular ways in which the making of the doll/child figures happened – the process of making – I raise issues around student agency, cultural memory, local knowledge and school learning.

## Points of fixing in the semiotic chain

The analysis of the children's 3D figures is situated within broader frames of practices and processes of making within the children's social and cultural worlds, which extend beyond the classroom into their homes. Thus the 3D figures can be viewed as 'concrete traces' of socio-cultural worlds of making. In discussing the child/doll figures, I have drawn on categories of analysis which have been used by scholars (Dell 1998, 2004; Nel and Leibhammer 1998) in African art history. These categories pay attention to the material and formal characteristics of such objects, including shape, texture, adornments, weight and height. They also focus on their symbolic functions in the social world.

In my analysis, the focus on these objects is on their transformations in relation to meaning as content and meaning as form. I examine the child/doll figures in terms of how children used them as points of fixing in the development of 'character' across different semiotic modes: how the child/doll figures are produced in the semiotic chain of transformations around 'character', from the initial conceptualisation of 'character', to the transformation of 'person' to 'character', from the transformation of 'character' to 'doll figure' in image and 3D to 'doll figure' as 'character' in a play or prose narrative. This analysis draws on Jewitt's (2002) analysis of how the entity 'character' is reshaped in the shift from page to screen. Using the example of multi-modal transformation of the novel *Of Mice and Men* to CD-ROM, she shows how when students read the book, they read to imagine the characters, their motivations, emotions, appearance and voice. This foregrounds their identification with the moral dilemmas of the characters. In working with the CD-ROM, the narrative, the characters, their motivations and relations are reshaped: the descriptions of the characters are supplied, and much of the imaginative work demanded by book reading is provided by the images. The CD-ROM reading of character does not engage with issues of morality or identification: rather, it prepares students to take the examination. Clearly, the move from page to screen has important implications for the teaching of 'character' and more broadly, the teaching of literature.

The child/doll figures are pivotal in the representation and communication of 'character' in this project: they speak back to the initial conceptualisation of 'person' into 'character' into 2D drawings, and speak forward to the 2D drawings, dialogues and plays which the children made after they had constructed these figures. Thus the focus of the investigation is to establish the affordances of the 3D child/doll figures in the semiotic chain from the perspective of meaning as both content and form.

I have paid more attention to elements of an ethnographic-style method in this chapter to provide a deeper sense of the history of the communicative practices in which the multimodal texts are being produced. This has involved adding the dimension of practices (in the sense understood by New

Literacy Studies) to the study of the texts produced, in order to understand more fully what these texts mean to those who made them, and how these texts fit into the practices of their lives (Barton and Hamilton 1998). Through interviewing the participants, I have paid specific attention to how the children, as sign-makers, reflect on and perceive their textual products and processes of making. The interpretations offered here are an attempt to bring together material, social and representational processes and practices in order to illuminate the role of children's culture-making in consciousness and its expression.

## The Olifantsvlei 'Fresh Stories' Project

The school is situated in the semi-rural district of Eikenhof outside Johannesburg, was formerly a mission school serving the children of local farm workers who lived as tenants on white-owned farms in the area. The school was converted in the early 1990s into a state school and now caters primarily for the needs of children who live in informal settlements nearby. These are children from poor families with parents, guardians or caregivers who are variously employed, unemployed, or migrants from neighbouring states in search of work on the Witwatersrand. Many of these children come from female, single-headed households, with few men around. Some of the children do not live with adults, but in child-headed households with brothers and sisters who care for them. Many of the children live in 'mkukus' or 'shacks' on small plots of land with no sanitation but some electricity. Living conditions for many of these children are extremely hard: aside from the child grant of R170, there is no social welfare for the poor and these children suffer from various forms of deprivation, neglect and malnutrition.

The children are multilingual speakers of local and foreign African languages. The school has chosen a 'straight for English' language policy in which English is the main language of teaching, learning and literacy from Grade 1 (in spite of progressive multilingual language-in-education policies in place). Although the chosen medium of instruction in this school from Grade 1 is English, in the 'Fresh Stories' project, children could work through any language they wished, including Zulu, Sotho, Tswana and English. This was quite difficult for the teachers to accept as they had taken the decision to focus on English as the target language of teaching and learning. However, as the project was in the nature of a pedagogical 'innovation', they agreed to go along with a multilingual approach.

The teachers were accustomed to providing scaffolding and direction for all learning activities in this school. The intention in this project, however, was to create a more relaxed and playful environment for making, which would allow the children to respond to the creative tasks with little or no intervention from teachers. The purpose of this was to construct within the constraints of school 'an unpoliced zone' in order to investigate the choices the children would make in terms of the 'stuff' which was to hand – their resources for representation – and their interests within the specific social context of making. In order to provide a stimulus for inventing stories, the children were asked to think of someone in their homes, neighbourhoods or streets who interested them, and who could become a 'character' in a story which they would create later on as a whole class. The idea was that the class would invent, through various multimodal transformatory processes, a cast of well-developed characters which would form the basis of ongoing playmaking, storytelling and story writing.

After the children had 'fixed' on a particular person, they were asked to act out how this person moved, walked, talked, laughed, sat down, and ate supper. Through dramatic action, the 'person' began evolving into a 'character'. They were then asked to draw 2D figures of the character and write something about this character in any language they wished. In the next stage of the process, the children were to make 3D figures of their characters in class. Their teachers made a papier mâché mixture for this purpose, but according to the children, 'the mixture flopped and our characters turned into puddles'. At this point, the children turned to their teachers and said, 'Don't worry, we'll make our own', and over the next few days, many of them brought into class a collection of 3D doll/child figures and cardboard cut-out figures which they had made at home. These doll/child figures were then used as puppet characters in a number of live performances, including dialogues and plays which they subsequently improvised in class. At the end of the process, the children were asked to write any story about their child/doll figures in any language they wished.

## The doll/child figures as socio-cultural manifestation

In this section, I compare the features of the contemporary doll/child figures which the children produced to 'traditional' fertility doll/child figures of the Southern African region in order to gain a deeper understanding of the children's uses of materiality, creativity and mutation of aesthetic form within culturally and historically situated practices of representation. Even though I refer in the analysis to 'traditional dolls' and compare these to 'contemporary dolls', 'tradition' as I have pointed out in Chapter 2, is a highly contested concept. Rather, my analysis reconceptualises doll-making on a continuum of making: all the different dolls which have been made are not in a binary relation between 'traditional' and 'contemporary' but are viewed *as points of fixing* in the ongoing semiotic chain of child/ doll making throughout history. Thus the comparisons made are between different examples of dolls in the semiotic chain of doll-making culture located within particular historical moments and communicative practices. Such communicative practices have developed conventions around what constitutes particular genres of 'dolls' within specific moments and contexts. I argue that the children's doll figures form part of the ongoing semiotic chain of social, cultural and aesthetic practices around fertility doll/child figures which have existed in Southern Africa for hundreds of years and which continue to exist in some communities today. Their evolving uses and forms are as fluid as the individuals and cultures they represent (Dell 2004: 50). In terms of their material, aesthetic and symbolic characteristics – their internal and external characteristics, their use of materials, external adornments and their overall design – they show remarkable similarities as well as significant differences to the grammar of such fertility child figures. The symbolic resonance of materials in 'traditional' fertility doll/child figures is echoed in the children's choices and use of the representational resources available to them in their home and community contexts, as well as in their processes of making. This social semiotic analysis thus provides a way of reading the doll/child figures against shifting backdrops of cultural memory and communicative practices which have been reflected in material solutions arising out of specific contexts of use, interests and historical moments. These layers of association are revealed through the form the figures take, the materials from which they are made and the words with which they are associated in the semiotic chain. They are also revealed through the children's reflections on the processes of making.

## *Definition of fertility doll/child figures*

The term 'fertility dolls' or 'child figures' refers to small objects with anthropomorphic forms, usually made by women for girls' and women's use in a range of contexts and domains relating to women's fertility, girls' initiation rituals, child rearing and marriage rituals. Their symbolism in form and materials is talismanlike, suggestive and affective (Nel and Leibhammer 1998). As this genre of culture-making emerges from female domains and relates to intimate areas of female identities and fertility, their uses in puberty and adolescent initiation practices have been kept secret from public scrutiny. As pointed out by Dell (1998), these objects are 'polyvalent', fulfilling multiple symbolic functions: as objects of play by girl children in the same way as children play with dolls the world over, as fertility charms, and as figures that have magical powers to act as 'evocations of the child' in fertility, puberty and marriage rituals in which the dolls function as intermediate between living and dead – between women and their powers to reproduce. Such dolls have been granted magical and metaphoric powers, acting 'as ciphers' through which a wished-for child or ancestral soul can pass through and enter into her owner's womb.

Dell (1998) has pointed out that since the 1980s, Ndebele costume dolls, which grew out of the more personal 'fertility dolls', have become highly popular tourist items, associated both with Ndebele 'traditional' values and costumes, and with a more generalised South Africa traditionalist identity. Nettleton *et al.* (2003) have noted the appearance of blond, Western-type Barbie dolls decorated with beadwork in recognisably ethnic forms and designs. These dolls do not seem to have been more generally adopted either for indigenous use or for the tourist market.

## Shapes

Southern African doll/child figures across regions and communities usually share a cylindrical or conical shape and are abstract, rather than figurative, in form. This can be clearly seen in the cylindrical shape of the Tsonga-Shangane doll in Figure 5.1, and in the conical shape of the Ndebele *umndwana* (child figure) in Figure 5.2. These primary forms which allude to women as receptacles or containers, result from the female body and dress forms which characterise the way women clothe themselves, for example, the shape made by Ndebele women who wrap their beaded blankets or wear conical rings around their necks in Ndebele style dress (Fig. 5.2). Their internal and external characteristics are achieved through multiple forms of layering: the conical and cylindrical shapes of the dolls are produced through the use of an inner core around which is folded and draped in stylised systems of multiple layerings, various types of cloth material and adornments. The inner cores are usually constructed from grass, reeds, bottles, gourds, calabashes, wild oranges, tins and wood. The containers such as the wild oranges and gourds are filled with talisman-like powders and seeds, then wrapped with different cloths, and finally adorned with glass beads, seeds, grasses, plant fibres, safety pins, metal and leather.

It is important to point out that the doll/child figures are represented as female adults, capable of procreation. They do not take the form of babies or children, like many Western-style dolls, although they evoke the idea of the potential child in how they are used as playthings and fertility charms.

The majority of doll/child figures made by the Olifantsvlei children were conical in shape and abstract in form. This effect was achieved through the use of plastic and glass bottles associated with the food and drink in domestic settings, namely cold drink (Sprite, Virgin and Coke) and cooking oil bottles (Figs 5.3, 5.4, 5.5, 5.6). In one doll, which was made entirely out of paper and plastic, the conical shape was achieved through cutting out a cardboard shape which when turned, formed a conical shape in an abstract and highly suggestive way. Another doll had a more figurative body shape: it was constructed out of a pair of sticks for the legs around which was moulded in an elaborate set of ties, folds and knots, an old stocking. This doll had a more defined body shape that emphasised large buttocks and large breasts moulded in counterpoint to one another.

*Figure 5.1*
Doll, Tsonga-Shangane, South Africa, Standard Bank African Art Collection (Wits Art Galleries)

## ***Weight and height***

The bottle interiors of the Olifantsvlei dolls had different degrees of weightiness. Some bottles were empty; others were filled with materials like foam chips, sand and stones in varying proportions. The weight of the dolls enabled them to remain standing solidly upright facing the viewer, a singular characteristic of all the dolls made. In the same way that the containers of the traditional dolls (wild oranges, tins, gourds) were often filled with talisman-like powders and seeds, the detailed attention by the children to the range of materials gathered to fill the interiors, points to evidence of their 'interests', both functional and symbolic, in relation to this aspect of doll-making. In terms of the height of the dolls, they were all more or less the same height, with a few variations. The height of 25 cms was determined by the choice of the size of cooldrink bottle: one doll made from a plastic cooking-oil bottle was slightly taller than the rest. However, like their ancestors, all the children's dolls could be described as small objects with few variations in size.

*Figure 5.2*
*Umndwana* (child figure), Ndebele, South Africa, Standard Bank African Art Collection (Wits Art Galleries)

### *Exterior attachments: heads, arms and breasts*

In the conventions established around the making of child/doll figures, heads were made in a variety of ways, including the use of stoppers adorned with beads or clay (Fig. 5.2). In the Olifantsvlei figures, heads were constructed out of scrunched up newspaper covered in stretch knit cloth or fabric rolled into a ball and attached by wire, string, glue or fabric to the neck of the bottles (Fig. 5.5). One doll had a piece of cloth cut into shreds resembling hair. In traditional figures, arms were usually made out of clay, strings of beads, or reeds, if they were made at all (Figs 5.1 and 5.2). In the children's dolls, they used nails, dowel sticks and twigs inserted into the bottles to suggest arms (Fig. 5.5). In traditional doll figures, breasts are rarely defined except in the clay figures and more abstractly represented through beads, for example. However, in the children's doll figures, there is marked attention paid to more figurative representations of breasts. One doll, wrapped in several cloths suggesting layers of blankets, looks like a baby but on lifting up the blankets, a pair of fully developed breasts are

*Figure 5.3*
Contemporary doll figure made by Dumisani. Plastic bubblewrap, plastic bag, glass bottle, twigs

revealed, centrally defined and prominent, which have been 'hidden' beneath the clothing. The boundaries between 'baby', 'girl' and 'woman' remain fluid. Another doll made from an artfully-wrapped woman's stocking has clearly defined breasts made from two stones covered with stocking (Fig. 5.5 (left)). The absence and presence of breasts, and the different ways in which they are defined, shaped and revealed, are evidence of social and cultural attitudes towards breasts and the female body, as well as marking the dolls as adolescent and adult female figures.

### *Use of fabric*

In traditional doll figures, the inner conical or cylindrical cores are usually covered in various types of cloth in earth colours. In styles of multilayering, different adornments are then attached to the cloth. According to Nel and Leibhammer (1998), the use of cloth firmly locates the tradition and practices around doll-making in the domain of women. The wrapping of the inner core with folds of cloth is highly symbolic of the union of male and female principles: the female cloth envelops the male phallic core in a symbolic representation of the procreative act.

The use of a rich variety of cloth in different textures, weaves, weights and colours, and folded in different ways, is a salient feature of the Olifantsvlei dolls. The range of cloth and the choices made regarding texture, design, colour and style of folds reveal a high level of care and interest in fashion styles and the aesthetics of cloth, which take established genres of doll-making into new arenas and redefine the female form. The use of women's stockings to symbolise a 'second skin' (Fig. 5.5 (left)), the use of fake fur in zebra stripes to cover a stylised body shape of prominent buttocks and breasts, the use of plastic bubblewrap brilliantly folded to suggest a billowing dress (Fig. 5.3), the use of different cloths (Figs 5.4 and 5.5), lace, socks, old duvet covers and dishcloths, in hues of blue, red, black, green, brown and white for 'doeks' and other head coverings (Fig. 5.6), suggest that the children had many fabric resources 'to hand' in their environment from which to select the particular cloth that they wanted. The use of fresh, clean cloth on the dolls is rare: they are mostly wrapped in waste pieces of cloth which have been refashioned into the desired shape and style (Fig. 5.6).

Although hand- or machine-sewn seams on the dolls are rare, the varieties of ways in which the cloth has been wrapped can be linked to the varied twists and folds which rural and cosmopolitan African women invent for the use of cloth as forms of body clothing and headdress. In other words, the use and shaping of cloth on the dolls in its various forms can be located within historical and cultural milieux in which cloth in its multiple textures and colours, intricate wraps and folds, defines identity, status and style within local communities as well as on the catwalks of contemporary African haute couture.

### *Use of adornments and face markings*

Whereas a key feature of 'traditional' Southern African dolls is the use of varied forms of adornment such as glass beads, ostrich shells, safety pins, coins, badges, buttons, chains and elaborate beadwork designs which reflect specific regional influences (Figs 5.1 and 5.2), the children's doll figures had relatively few adornments. One doll (Fig. 5.5 (right)) was decorated with two necklaces: a plastic colourful necklace for a little girl with punched out starfish and conical shell shapes, and a second black bead necklace distinctly African in style. This doll had 'ears' symbolised by small brass safety pins on each side of the head. The children used a variety of marks in ballpoint or felt-tip pen to signal facial features, including eyes, noses and mouths. Some faces had no markings at all and one doll was headless (Fig. 5.4).

*Figure 5.4*
Contemporary doll figure made by Tsepang. Fabric, mattress stuffing, sand, plastic bottle, wire

### *Processes and practices of making the doll/child figures*

Interviews were conducted with eight children who made dolls to investigate in more depth the processes of making, including:

- who made the doll/child figures;
- how they were made;
- where the children obtained the materials for making them;
- who the dolls 'represented' for them;
- how the children had used the doll/child figures and for what purposes.

It emerged from their responses that in every case, an adult woman – a mother, a grandmother, an aunt or a neighbour – had helped the child in the making of the doll. This help took different forms: in some cases, the

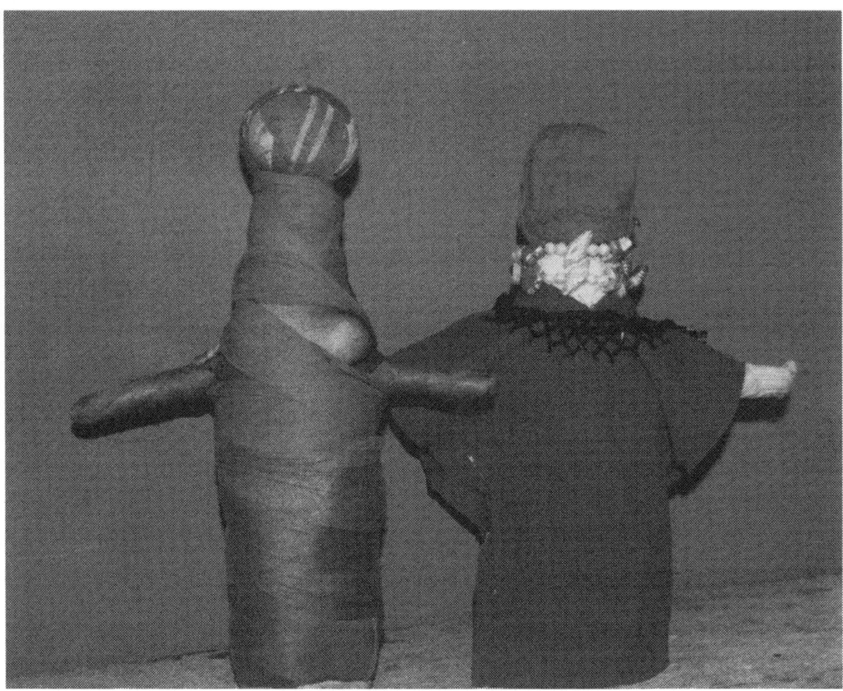

*Figure 5.5* Contemporary doll figures made by Busi (left) and Sonti (right). Busi's doll: plastic bottle, women's stockings, sticks, stones, crayon, fabric. Sonti's doll: fabric, plastic bottle, sand, coloured shell necklace, African bead necklace, sticks

child and the grandmother or mother physically constructed the doll together. So, for example, in Figure 5.5 (right), the mother sewed the cloth and gave suggestions for the structure of the doll, and the child chose the cloth and adornments. In the case of the bubblewrap doll (Fig. 5.3), which was made by a boy, an aunt suggested to him that he make the doll out of plastic bags and showed him how to tie a plastic bag to give the impression of a doek around the head. In the case of a figurative doll figure made by a boy and his mother, the mother constructed the inner body shape emphasising breast and buttocks in a complex use of stocking ties and twigs, and then allowed her son to 'dress' her in a fake zebra fur skirt and top. In some cases, the children were emphatic about the fact that they made them 'themselves'. When I asked one girl who had made the stocking doll (Fig. 5.5 (left)), she said 'myself' and when asked how she learnt how to make such a doll, she replied, 'My granny from Lesotho taught me', adding that she had made three other dolls like this before. Another girl said, 'my mother from the

*Figure 5.6*
Contemporary doll figures made by Winnie and Palesa. Assorted fabrics, dishcloth, bottles, sand

Transkei' helped her to make her doll. This information is invaluable in coming to understand the social context of making such dolls within local households and clearly points to the continuing role of adult women in the processes of making. Significantly, no child mentioned that an adult man helped to make the doll. However, what is interesting are the clear shifts in gendered patterns of making at the level of the children: several dolls were made by boy children with mothers or aunts acting as mentors in passing on knowledge, skills and practices regarding a formerly strictly female cultural domain.

Another important point arising from the children's reports on the process of making is the collaborative nature of the making: how children knew where and how to recruit cultural and community knowledge in the family or neighbourhood in order to realise their needs. Through various forms of collaboration with adults in this kind of cultural activity, children and adults are engaging in the transformation of semiotic resources, in the making of new signs. Children and adults are building on their capacities for shared problem solving, creativity and communication. These learning activities are rooted in the 'deep knowledge' of communicative practices existing in families and communities, in urban and rural mixes, which finds its expression in the continuities and transformations of ideas around what constitutes doll/child figure making within this place.

In discussing who the doll/child figures were based on, it appears that each child had named the child figure after a person close to them, for example, 'Gogo' ('my grandmother'), 'Mpho' ('my sister'), 'Pinky' ('one of the girls who lives in the squatter camp who doesn't go to school'), 'Disebo' ('a friend who lives in Freedom Park'). When asked about how they might use such doll/child figures, children said things like, 'I wash them and feed them', 'My mother told me to use them as children', and 'It is my baby doll and my mother'. When I asked them if their doll figures were the 'same or different to Barbie dolls', they were quite clear about their differences and provided elaborate descriptions of how Barbies were different from theirs, 'in the hands, the necks, the shape of the bodies, in the fingers, the hair, the head and the feet'. These comments provide evidence for ways in which the child/doll figures become invested with psychological and symbolic value: in playing with these objects, the children act out wishes, desires, fantasies and anxieties. Their comments also point to degrees of self-awareness and reflection, of consciousness 'speaking out', around the processes of making and its representation.

## Taking the ordinary and making the extraordinary: the aesthetics of waste

In interviewing the children on their use of materials, it became evident that they had consciously looked for materials to suit their needs and had made careful decisions, sometimes with an adult, about how to use these materials. The child who had shaped a doll figure from folds fashioned from one large piece of discarded dishcloth (Fig. 5.6 (left)) told me she had gone into the bush or 'veld' to look for materials and had found this cloth. Another child told me he had found the bottle for his conical shaped inner core 'in a rubbish bin outside the disco'. No child had the means to purchase any new materials for making the dolls: they had found the resources, the 'waste' in their environments and had reshaped them according to their affective, symbolic and aesthetic interests. What these figures reveal is the dynamic relationship between creativity, innovation and resources: 'resources' take on different values and meanings in different contexts of use. A discarded plastic bag on a rubbish dump becomes a doek: that which cannot be eaten is fashioned into a doll. A safety pin becomes an ear, a button an eye, a nail an arm and a stone a breast. The point is that these children had no other choice but to forage in the veld and through the rubbish dumps around them to find what they needed. Such limits can be very generative: these children were able to see potential in the ordinary and transform it into the extraordinary.

These 3D figures illustrate the hybridity and fluidity of contemporary urban cultural life in South African cities and the degree to which cultural and generic transformation has taken place at multiple levels. At the level of 'making', it is usually women who make such dolls but in this project, boys participated in the making of their own dolls. The established boundaries around what constitutes 'child fertility dolls' within ethnic and gender classifications have collapsed and in this process, the 'traditional' in all its multiplicity of forms and materiality is redesigned into the 'contemporary' using available contextual materials. These doll/child figures illustrate how individuals have many layers of representational resources available to them, not only from one culture, but also from many cultures. As Hamilton (1998: 26) has noted in her work on African women's material culture as markers of identity, the analysis of the production of material culture has the potential to change the way in which discussions about identity are framed: material culture 'speaks to identity as at once conservatively continuous with the past and as creatively innovative, as bounded and as porous, as transportable and as rooted.' The children's process of remaking is not reproductive or imitative, but innovative and transformative, both of the objects, which are extending the 'grammar' of doll-making culture, and in relation to the children's identities.

One of the questions we might ask of the doll figures is how to account for their beauty, a beauty which comes from the found materials of poverty, what in some people's terms might be thought of as waste, as ugliness. In an essay on rethinking beauty in relation to aesthetics in Africa, Nuttall shows the integral association of beauty with a form of largely socially defined ugliness and abjection:

> Beauty is to be found at the limits of the ugly, since it is the ugly which has so often been the sign under which the African has been read . . . beauty always stands in intimate relation to ugliness, both in Africa and elsewhere, though this configuration of the beautiful and the ugly has often been suppressed in Western-based philosophies of aesthetics.
>
> (Nuttall 2006: 8)

Malaquais (2006) writes about the aesthetics of waste in the post-colonial city Douala, Cameroon, where the first work of public art, a sculpture, is made entirely of waste. Here, beauty is born from the distress of the city. Malaquais quotes the writer, Issa Diabate of Cote d'Ivoire, on 'matter' in the city:

> The city is born of its subjection to matter . . . Like all life, it rises from things rotting. Part body-part, part machine, like living beings, it creates odours and excrement and waste. From these, ideas and sensibilities are born – a language of the city.
>
> (Diabate 1999, Trans Malaquais)

In terms of the doll figures, it seems that the idea of making something beautiful mattered to some children and was a case of uncertainty for others. For the child who made the bubblewrap doll, beauty is a question of materiality and form: it has everything to do with the materiality of his medium, how to manipulate the small piece of bubblewrap in ways suggestive of a caftan-robe, how to twirl the plastic bag around the bottlehead to suggest an African head scarf. And how to make sure that it all stays in place on the long bus ride to school. There is a wonderful certainty about the way the stocking doll stands in the world, confident of her beauty. For other children, whether the dolls turned out beautiful was unpredictable: the doll figure made from filthy, bloodied scraps of cloth garnered from the veld (Fig. 5.6 (left)) is hauntingly beautiful in its abjectness: its beauty is to be found at the limits of the ugly.

## Culture, circulation and the capacity to aspire

Mbembe (2002), in his analysis of the changing forms of urban life in post-colonial cities in Africa, refers to practices of 'circulation' of cultural forms brought about through global media, capital and migration. He refers to Johannesburg as a place of 'circulation' in which multiple modernities converge to produce new cultural and aesthetic forms. The doll-making project exemplifies such processes of circulation. In its communal and inter-generational processes of making, and in the imaginative use of recycled urban waste materials found on rubbish dumps in informal settlements in this contemporary African city, signs of poverty and distress are transformed into objects of beauty and flamboyance. Drawing on the work of Appadurai (2002), I would claim that through the process and practice of making objects such as these, which have local cultural voice, the children's capacities to have and cultivate 'voice' have been strengthened. Through the delicate twists and folds of plastic bags and old cloths, the meticulous shaping of breasts, arms, bodies and heads with sticks, stones and bottles, the children are using cultural forms to display their 'capacity to aspire', thereby placing futurity rather than pastness at the centre of their meaning-making.

## Shifting contexts of use in the semiotic chain

In this section I return to the Olifantsvlei 'Fresh Stories' Project to focus on how the dolls were used by some children as 'points of fixing' in the semiotic chain. This chain led from the initial conceptualisation, 'Think of a person you know who can become a character in a play' (Stage 1), to the transformation of that imagined person into a 'character' who is drawn and written about (Stage 2), to the transformation of the drawn and written-about character into a 3D doll figure (Stage 3), to the transformation of the 3D doll figure into a character who performs in a play (Stage 4), to the transformation of the performing 3D figure as 'character' into a character who is written about in a narrative (Stage 5). I have chosen two examples to give readers a sense of the range of semiotic objects produced in this chain.

### Busi's semiotic chain

Busi, a Grade 2 girl, imagined a 'person' in Stage 1 whom she transformed into a 'character' called 'mother' in her drawing and writing in Stage 2 (Fig. 5.7). Her 'mother' character in her writing is named 'Nthabiseng'. She is someone who cooks porridge 'after school':

> *The name of my mother is Nthabiseng is my mother Nthabiseng His cook after school His cook a porrige*

She depicted her 'mother' in a figurative way, conventionally Western rather than abstract in form, showing her head, earrings and hair, her torso, her clothing and her arms and legs. In Stage 3 of the transformation process, she went home and made her 3D doll figure out of wrapped stockings (Fig. 5.5 (left)). This 'character' is distinctly different both in form and content to her previous representation of 'mother' as 'character'. The 'mother' drawn in Stage 2, with earrings and clothing and a recognisable figurative form, has been transformed into a highly abstract, minimal form, constructed out of a bottle, two stones and women's stockings. 'Mother' as 'character' is different: she has been remade. Busi, significantly, chose not to use her 'mother' doll figure in a play in Stage 4 of the process. 'Mother' as 'character' in a play simply does not appear. In Stage 5, however, Busi produced a new drawing of a different 'character' called Dineo, and wrote a story about her 'baby' whom she named 'Dineo' (Fig. 5.8). The period of time between the first piece of writing and the second was two months.

In Busi's 2D drawings, 3D doll figure and written texts, her points of fixing reveal interesting 'slippage' in her semiotic chain. Her semiotic chain starts, in the sense that she produces the 'first sign' with a 2D figurative drawing of 'her mother', accompanied by a written text in which she writes about 'her mother' who 'cooks porrige' and who is named Nthabiseng. Busi then makes a 3D abstract doll figure at home on her own, who emerges as a complex representation of female fertility: the 3D figure is simultaneously herself, her mother as a fertile mother, herself as a fertile mother, and her 'wished for' baby. This fertile mother (herself) symbolically and magically gives birth to a child who becomes Busi's 'child' in her written story, in which Busi tells the story of 'her baby Dineo'.

At the level of style, the drawing of the baby Dineo is similar in style to the first drawing of her mother. Busi's shift in styles of representation from 2D to 3D is from figurative to abstract forms, illustrating the generic conventions Busi has been taught or has assimilated around drawing human

*Figure 5.7* First drawing and written text by Busi

figures (as mainly figurative) and making doll figures (as mainly abstract). In the realm of the symbolic and fantasy, Busi takes on the role of the mother, gives birth to her own child and through this act of making, holding and viewing (both the doll as material and the doll as child), Busi becomes the agent who perpetuates the generation. In the transformations from initial conceptualising of a person to a character to a doll figure to a doll character in a narrative, a doll can become that which you love which was once part of yourself. The child/doll figure is made by Busi to serve her own desires, fantasies and interests in the semiotic chain: in the transformation from her initial focus on her mother as 'person' and 'character' to the focus on the baby Dineo and herself, Busi uses her doll to fulfil its symbolic

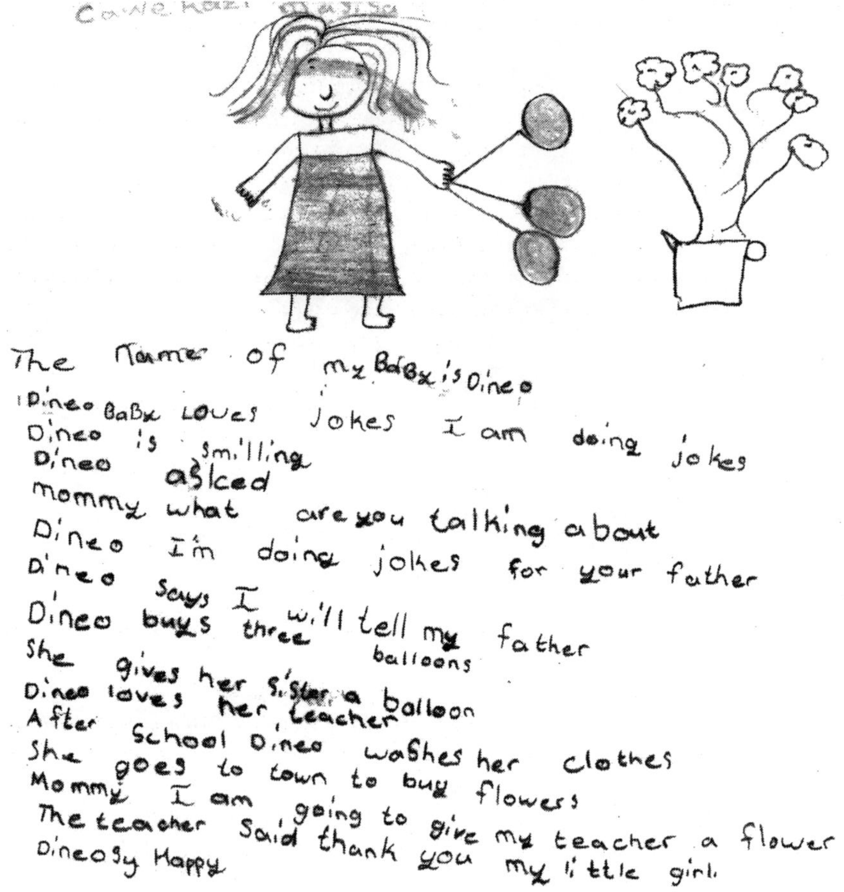


*Figure 5.8* Final drawing and written text by Busi

function which is to create another body in which the spirit of the child would evolve. And in the sensual act of holding and perceiving the object she has made, literally and symbolically, she re-imagines what it is and what it is to become.

## *Sonti's semiotic chain*

Sonti's doll/child figure, whom she names Ntswaki (Fig. 5.5 (right)), is a syncretic mix of the traditional African doll figure and the contemporary. With safety pins for ears, a traditional African black bead necklace and a Taiwanese pink, green and purple, plastic seashell necklace wound around her neck, Ntswaki straddles the African and the Western, the local and the global, the past, the present and future. She is child, plaything, woman and mother. Sonti uses this doll/child figure in an improvised dialogue in Sotho:

*Sonti:* Lebitso la hae ke Ntswaki. Ntswaki o ne a rata ho bapala le bana. Jwale a itebala a fihla bosiu. Ntate a ba a mo fihlele pele. Mme ke hona a kenang ka tlung.
**Her name is Ntswaki. Ntswaki likes to play with the children. She used to be relaxed while she played and used to come back home late. Her husband would get home first. It's then that the mother, Ntswaki, came into the house.**

*Father/Husband:* (*in a deep voice*) Mme o tswa kae ka nako e?
**Mother/wife, where do you come from at this time?**

*Ntswaki:* (*trembling*) A . . . a . . . a . . . /nna ke ne ke ilo bapala le bana.
**A . . . ah . . . ah . . . I went to play with the children.**

*Father/Husband:* Why o rata ho bapala le bana?
**Why do you like to play with children?**

*Ntswaki:* Nna ke rata bana.
**I like children.**
(*A ba a setse a mo mathisa.*) **(He chases her out of the house.)**

*Father/Husband:* Mme, why o itebala hore o tlo pheha?
**Mother/wife, why do you forget that you have to cook?**

*Ntswaki:* Ha ke a itebala. Ke ne ke tlile. Ke ne ke nahana hore wena ha wa mphihlela pele. A ba a re.
**I am not relaxed. I came here. I thought that you would not be home before me. (She said.)**

*Father/Husband:* O-
**Oh.**

*Ntswaki:* A ba a re nna ha ke sa tla hlola ke bapala le bana.
**I'm not going to play with the children again.**

Sonti's dialogue plays with the theme of marriage, children and patriarchy. The doll/child figure, Ntswaki, is out playing with 'the children' and neglects to come home in time to cook supper for her husband. He instructs her to 'stop playing' and to 'start cooking', in other words, to stop being a 'child' and take on the role of a 'woman/wife'. Ntswaki challenges him initially but this turns into submission. Ntswaki is simultaneously a child-bride, a plaything, a mother and a wife. In this extract, Sonti takes further the iconic power of the male and female principles, symbolised in the doll figures, in a self-reflexive and playful enactment of the notions of play: the consequences of being a child and a bride are that the time for 'play' is brief as you enter into patriarchy, marriage and motherhood.

It seems clear from Busi's and Sonti's use of the doll/child figures for writing and for dialogue, that these 3D figures provide an important identity function in the semiotic chain. Through their physicality – their shape, weight, density and use of materials – they become embodiments of 'ideas' and 'images' of characters in the children's imaginations that they become attached to and identify with. They can be felt, touched, held, gazed at, moved from place to place and situated in different settings. The very flatness of 2D drawings is contrasted with the fullness in space of the 3D doll figures. In the act of drawing the characters, the makers are viewers; in the act of holding the dolls, the makers are both viewers and bearers of their own creation. In this act of 'holding', the characters become embodied and take on a different identity for the holders. It is for these reasons that I think the 3D figures, from the perspective of both materiality and their domains of provenance, were absolutely central in shaping the children's narratives by providing them with something literally to hold on to, and to take responsibility for, in the making of meaning.

## Creativity as variations on a theme

Multimodal pedagogies stretch already existing creativity in unexpected, unpredictable ways. How does this occur in pedagogical environments? Hofstadter's theory of creativity provides some insights into the process: 'Making variations on a theme is really the crux of creativity' (Hofstadter 1985: 233). When a concept enters a new domain, it starts migrating and developing in ways which are unexpected and unanticipated. Another crucial idea in this theory is the notion of 'slippage' in which concepts have a way of 'slipping' into one another, with unpredictable results. Concepts, in their very structure, contain 'slippability'. The most productive form of slippage is 'nondeliberate yet nonaccidental' which permeates our mental processes, and is 'the very crux of fluid thought.' (Hofstadter 1985: 237). Creativity is also produced when the context changes: one comes to view the phenomenon in new ways, which in itself generates new images.

In working with different modes of representation in semiotic chains, each mode has the potential to produce multiple variations on a concept. By varying different modes, introducing and adding new modes to existing modes in infinite chains, a huge number of variations on a concept are made possible. Recontextualising the concept in new domains allows it to migrate from familiar domains and attach itself to new conceptual territory, which in turn produces new variations on the concept and subsequently, new texts.

The 'Fresh Stories' Project demonstrates this process at work: once the children had decided that the papier mâché was not working for them, they consciously chose a new context (their homes) in which to make their doll figures. In the making of doll figures in the home contexts, 'doll making' was framed by the participants (the children and their mothers, grandmothers and women informants) in terms of familiar concepts (traditional doll-making cultural practices). These practices form part of residual cultural memory and have conventions and styles that have been socially produced in African communities over many years. However, in the new context of production (making 3D figures in your home-setting for a school project on stories), what gets made is dependent on which materials for representation are available and how these materials will serve each doll-maker's interests. Working with environmentally available waste materials such as old plastic bags, bubblewrap, safety pins and old stockings takes the concept of 'doll making' into new conceptual territory, providing the makers with endless possibilities for variation on a 'traditional' doll theme. This is an instance of how 'fixing' works in the semiotic chain of continuities and innovations in doll/child figure-making culture.

The 'fixing' in terms of the semiotic chain of narrative is produced in a similar way. The idea of 'Make a character from your world' starts off as an initial conceptualising in the form of an imagined 'person' who is transformed into a 'character' in a 2D drawing and written narrative, then transformed into a 3D-doll figure which has weight and substance. In the act of making, the 3D figure slips in and out of an intertextual response to the familiar 2D drawing and writing (looking backwards in the chain) into new conceptual territory (pointing forwards in the chain). Such a process reflects 'slippability' in the ways in which certain ideas about the character get dropped, migrate, and new ideas are picked up on and developed in endless cycles of variations on the theme. Some of these variations involve conscious choices on the part of the sign-maker but choices can be made *unconsciously* in the act of making. Different forms of desire can motivate such unconscious choices. Busi's variations migrated from writing and drawing her mother, to making a doll figure that took on a symbolic life as simultaneously herself, her mother, herself as mother, and her baby. This polyvalent object gives 'birth' to baby Dineo, who becomes the main subject of her final story, in which Busi evolves into the mother of baby Dineo. The point to be made is although the object appears to be 'fixed' in the sense that it materialises into what appears to be a static text, the meanings attached to the text, from the perspective of both form and content, are unstable and fluid within the semiotic chain.

## Conclusion

The main focus of this chapter has been on the products and practices of making the 3D doll/child figures by Grade 1 and 2 children and their relationship to other points of fixing in the semiotic chain set up by the 'Fresh Stories' project. Through an exploration of the children's transformation and recontextualisation of culturally and historically situated practices surrounding the representation of such doll/child figures and their symbolic meanings, we are able to gain a deeper understanding into the relations between creativity, multimodal pedagogies, resources for representation, and learning. It seems that pedagogies that consciously work to structure and stimulate variations on concepts or themes stretch creativity. Multimodal pedagogies have a capacity for slippage: they enable learners to play with nameless and wordless concepts and 'fix' them in multiple variations of shapes, colours, patterns, weights, densities, cloths, words, images. This 'slippage' can brought about through play: through creating a healthy tension between regulated and free play in classrooms spaces.

Learners' choices of semiotic resources are determined to some extent by availability within the wider semiotic environment in which they move. However, the above examples demonstrate that what a child finally produces is influenced by when and how the child 'takes' agency in relation to his or her interests and needs around representation, and the degree of familiarity the child enjoys with the representational resources available. Some children exhibit more flexibility with certain resources than others do: Busi seems to have more flexibility and familiarity with the language, English, than Dumisani, the child who made the doll in Figure 5.3. Dumisani, however, shows flexibility with minimal resources: bubble-wrap, plastic bags and a Coke bottle. In terms of questions of 'value' it is possible, as many artists have shown, to make an effective, beautiful object out of minimal resources, if the maker has confidence, creativity and a 'deep knowledge' in that practice.

In relation to the taking of agency and its consequences, the Olifantsvlei 'Fresh Stories' project shows the potential for more 'slippage' between home, communities and schools in our context. The children's statement, 'Don't worry, we'll make our own', in response to the failure of the papier mâché mixture, can be read as a profound challenge to the authority of school ways of doing things which are alien and disconnected from children's worlds, histories and experiences of making. When given the chance to create their own objects at home, they drew on people close to them who had knowledge of such practices and who assisted them in the making. It seems clear that through this assertion of identity, cultural practices and community, these children are showing their teachers that their home environments need to be more valued for their potential to speak back to the school, and that through such synergies, important forms of learning and teaching can take place.

Chapter 6

# Multimodal pedagogies

## Instances of practice

### Introduction

The previous chapters have demonstrated how applying a multimodal social semiotic lens, in combination with an ethnographic perspective, provides a different way of 'seeing' children's texts, making their complexity and creativity visible in new ways. Such analyses help us to trace identity and social practice in the materiality of texts (Pahl and Rowsell 2006: 2). The analyses also help us to understand how modes work, their affordances, and how students can make use of different modes in their learning and reshaping of knowledge.

This chapter focuses more directly on multimodality and pedagogy. It investigates four instances of *multimodal pedagogies* in practice. In each case, it attempts to explain how teachers and students use 'mode/s' to extend and develop thinking and learning. In other words, it tries to understand how modes are being used, to what end and to what effect. Mapping how teachers and students actively work with modes and multimodality in their classrooms gives us a better understanding of the relationship between modes, pedagogy, knowledge and learning. It enables us to examine what multimodality has to offer as a pedagogic resource and how it can be used to improve learning.

### Multimodal pedagogies: use of the term

I use the term 'multimodal pedagogies' to refer to curriculum, pedagogy and assessment practices which focus on mode as a defining feature of communication in learning environments. In other words, there is a recognition that all acts of communication in classrooms are multimodal: there is no monomodal communication (Jewitt and Kress 2003). Modes are not neutral: modes have power in different communicative contexts. A mode is a *social* semiotic: modes have characteristic forms, affordances and distinctive ways of interacting with each other. Some modes are better than other modes for certain kinds of representational work. Each mode provides teachers and students with a range of semiotic resources from which to choose, and the *choice* from these available resources is made on the basis of the sign-maker's interests and the resources which are available. The classroom is itself a multimodal place with visual displays and the arrangement of furniture in space that realises particular discourses of English, for example (Jewitt 2005). All of these modes shape the production of curriculum knowledge and pedagogic practices that lead to learning. The relationship between modes and users is dynamic and transforming: modes change users and users change modes. In multimodal pedagogies, there is a recognition that the use of modes in classrooms is always the effect of the work of culture, history and power in shaping materials into resources for meaning-making. Pedagogic processes (including designing of texts) can be understood as the selection and configuration of the semiotic resources available in the classroom.

Multimodal pedagogies acknowledge learners as agentive, resourceful and creative meaning-makers who communicate using the communicative potential and multiple resources of their bodies and of their environment to interconnect. Learners engage with different modes differently: they have different relationships, histories and competencies in relation to modes. In multimodal pedagogies, there is a conscious awareness of the relationship between modes, learning and identity. Texts have to be understood as multimodal in order to reveal their depths. Attending to the full ensemble of communicative modes that are involved in classrooms enables a rich view of the complex ways in which policy and curriculum is mediated and articulated through classroom practices and the part played by culture, language and identity in this process.

Four examples of multimodal pedagogies are presented below. Each instance illustrates aspects of the above definition in practice. All the examples described are based on work by teachers and researchers in Johannesburg classrooms.

### *Instance of practice 1: synaesthesia in a university classroom: dancing the pathway of sound*

In a university classroom, two university lecturers, Kathleen Wemmer and Marion Drew (2004), are teaching a course, *Pathology of the Ear*, to a group of second-year audiology students. The work of an audiologist is multi-faceted: an audiologist is akin to a 'detective' who pieces together puzzles that explain why a patient is dizzy, or disabled by tinnitus. They are rehabilitators, inventors and healers (Jacobsen 2002: 54–5).

This second-year course is medically orientated and deals with pathologies which could result in hearing loss or damage to the auditory or vestibular systems. Understanding the basic anatomy of the auditory system is essential. The students tell their teachers that they are struggling to visualise a three-dimensional structure (the middle ear) that is represented two-dimensionally in their textbook diagrams. Their teachers give them a box and ask them to bring materials to class which are suitable to represent the anatomical structures found in the middle ear. In groups, they 'translate' the two-dimensional diagram into a three-dimensional structure model of the middle ear. They are guided through the process by their teachers who act as 'consultants', and by 'expert' peers who are able to negotiate the spatial relations of anatomical structures. Their next task is to investigate the inner ear. From their weekly journal work it becomes clear that students have grasped the anatomical structures that constitute the inner ear but do not understand how sound moves through the structure. Drawing on an arts-based approach, the teachers hire a hall for the afternoon and ask students to work in teams to 'dramatically depict how sound moves through the cochlea (inner ear)'. Students are provided with textbooks and posters as they collaborate on how to 'act out the pathway of sound' (Wemmer and Drew 2004: 6).

The traditional approach to the course has been highly didactic in structure, focused on the factual, medical nature of the course content, and the large amount of information that needs to be covered. The course has consisted of a series of lectures where students are provided with decontextualised, technical knowledge regarding pathologies of the ear, such as age of onset, presenting symptoms and disease process. According to Wemmer and Drew, the information was presented in a fairly tedious manner and students often failed to see the relevance of the information to their future working lives as practicing audiologists:

> Whilst this approach certainly does go some way towards addressing the issue of providing learners with the knowledge, it does not address the issue of cognition or metacognition. We have noticed that our final year learners struggled to apply knowledge of pathology clinically despite experience in hospital settings.
>
> (Wemmer and Drew 2004: 2)

They decide to take a new approach, using a pedagogy of multiliteracies (Cope and Kalantzis 2000) which offers them the opportunity to work with multimodality. Aware of how different modes and media can be used to teach different concepts and therefore enable different kinds of learning, they redesigned the course, aiming to create a 'working life' context within which students could apply their new knowledge. They aimed to take students out of the 'traditional pen and paper' approach to learning, into working with modes where 'anatomical facts and concepts were represented in a way which made them more accessible, less abstract and closer to anatomical reality' (Wemmer and Drew 2004: 9).

Students were encouraged to think of themselves as 'capable future audiologists'. They built models of the ear, wrote weekly journals, watched videos of surgery and critically discussed issues of access to such surgery in developing countries. They engaged with questions of 'truth' and its representation in relation to diseases of the ear: how diseases are represented in medical discourses, and how ordinary people see these diseases and 'talk' about them. They explored reactions of different cultural groups to deformity, asking questions about who has control over the pathology and treatment of otitis media, often associated with poor living conditions and common in children who are HIV-positive. They critically interrogated why Western models of medicine are taken for granted and the extent to which local, indigenous healing models are marginalised. In one assignment, students had to interview someone of the older generation and of another healing persuasion in order to research 'traditional' or 'folk' remedies for otitis media. Their final assignment was to design websites for laypersons (parents and spouses) on their chosen pathologies and put their work online. This involved them in navigating and constructing multiple discourses and genres. In evaluating students' examination papers, the external examiner commented on the marked increase from previous years in the students' ability to demonstrate a broad range of knowledge of audiological procedures, and to apply this to the real working world of the audiologist.

In this course, some important learning is taking place. Wemmer and Drew recognise that curriculum concepts or 'content' are produced and distributed in the complex interrelations working within and across multiple sign systems (images, words, symbols, artifacts, gestures, body movement), different temporalities and learners' own knowledges and resources. In this learning environment, knowledge is situated and embodied and the learner is constructed as agentive, critical and resourceful. There is also a clear approach to working with texts focusing on the relationship between design, multimodality and audience. The teachers are explicit about the fact that different modes offer different potentials for representation: some modes are better, more effective, for certain tasks than others.

One of the hallmarks of this pedagogy is the conscious use of synaesthesia, the activity of translation or transduction between modes and senses. Synaesthesia is described by Kress as follows:

> even where a particular medium is favoured, there is constant transition, translation, transduction between different modes – in the brain, even if not necessarily visible on paper or with other media or modes. It is important to insist on this constant work of translation, transduction, which takes place at a level in the brain beyond easy inspection – although we may 'catch ourselves' at times translating a sound into words, a string of words into colours, a smell into a tactile feeling, and so on.
>
> (Kress 1997a: 39)

In the redesigning of this course, the teachers were committed to 'translating' anatomical facts and concepts in a way which would make them 'more concrete and tangible for the students'. This involved working with materiality in different ways in versions of 'resemiotization' (Iedema 2003) where meaning-making accumulates different material realisations, producing different entities. In one example, students translated two-dimensional 'flat' drawings into three-dimensional tactile models which occupied space. In a vivid example of the use of synaesthesia as a pedagogic strategy, students were encouraged to experiment with 'dancing the pathway of sound'.

### *Instance of practice 2: photo-romans in a Catholic middle school: exploring multimodal cohesion*

The school discussed below is a well-resourced, co-ed Catholic day school in Johannesburg. The school population is culturally, racially, linguistically and religiously diverse. The majority of students are from middle-class families and bursaries are provided for 25 per cent of the children, many of whom are children of domestic workers working in the neighbourhood. This school was one of the first schools in South Africa to declare itself 'open' in the late 1970s in defiance of the segregated racial policies of the apartheid government. Once the school became multiracial and multicultural, teachers found that the apartheid curriculum was unworkable for them and decided to develop their own curriculum. Through its innovative interdisciplinary 'integrated studies' curriculum, the school has been a leader in the field of curriculum innovation. It has committed itself to the production of high-quality teaching and learning materials which are critical, engaged and 'local'.

The principal of the school, Colin Northmore, is an English teacher deeply committed to 'helping children to express what they know'. He has a special interest in film studies and ICT and was keen to develop a programme for his Grade 8 and 9 students which would develop their film literacy sufficiently to enable them to make a short (video) fiction film in Grade 10. He consulted with a professor in film studies from New York University, who suggested that the best way to become what he calls '*cinemate*' ('literate' in the cinema) is to understand how to tell a story through 'the visual', specifically how *visual narratives* work. This can be done by asking the question of any film: what do I learn about this story *without sound and without dialogue?*

It was suggested that students work in small groups to create photo-romans. Photo-romans, as one of the oldest forms of moving image, serve as an ideal introduction to the language of time-based media. A photo-roman (or cine-roman) is a film genre in which a story is told through a series of still photographs assembled into a kind of slide show. It can be with or without sound. The photo-roman is constructed around the frame, the basic building block of film, video and computer animation. To introduce students to this genre, the students watched a classic example of a photo-roman, *La Jetee* (The Jetty), a 28-minute black and white science fiction film made by Chris Markor in 1962. This post-nuclear war story is told using a series of optically printed photographs, taken with a Pentax camera, and assembled as a photo-montage. The pace is varied and there is no dialogue – only a narration consisting of a voice-over. (For similar projects in animated film and onscreen presentations with primary school children, see Burn and Parker 2003 and UKLA/QCA booklet 2005.)

The photo-roman project was conceptualised in three stages. The first stage would focus on developing students' competence in constructing a visual narrative without sound effects, music or dialogue. In the second stage, they would construct a visual narrative with sound effects and/or music. Only in the third and final stage, would they be allowed to introduce dialogue, as well as sound and music, into their photo-romans. Through this carefully controlled sequence, students would grapple with the key modalities of film: image, music, sound and dialogue – in that order. In producing an assemblage of their photos, starting with a rough sequence and leading to a final edited cut, students would learn how to edit their work and to place themselves in the dual position of viewers and makers.

Digital cameras, computers and a film-making programme – in this case, Microsoft Office Movie Maker – are required to complete this project. The school had two digital cameras which students shared. If digital cameras are not available, the same project can be carried out with disposable cameras and a slide projector: the photos are made into slides and projected through the slide projector.

To prepare the students to make their photo-romans, Northmore provided a range of stimulus activities. They watched *La Jetee* and analysed it in terms of the sequencing of the plot, the use of icons, motifs, sound and music to create atmosphere, the use of perspective and viewpoint to hold viewers' attention. They discussed the effects of black and white, and colour, as digital cameras can be adjusted for black and white or colour. They were introduced to basic photographic/film techniques such as lighting, camera angles and types of shot including close-ups, high-, medium- and low-angle shots. Students were advised about point of view and told, 'Don't take every picture from the same space.' They were shown how to make a storyboard and the link between a storyboard and the final product. Finally, they were shown interesting examples of students' photo-romans from the previous year.

The photo-roman project was a cross-curriculum project, located across ICT and English. It took ten weeks to complete, working two hours a week. It was compulsory for all students. It was assessed and students had to write a reflective piece on the project after completion. The task was structured within time and space limits:

- The film could not be less than two minutes and not more than four.
- The story had to take place within the location of the school.

- Students were given a broad scenario: *You arrive at school one day and it's a day like none other. Tell this story.*
- Students worked in groups of four: one person as editor, one person as cameraperson, one person as director and one person who brings it together electronically.
- Everyone collaborates on the story. The group has to agree on the story.

### *Reflection on the project*

This project is now into its third year or 'cycle'. Over 50 photo-romans have been created. The school as location has proved to be a very generative and containing metaphor. Stories have been about the loneliness of school, a stranger (alien, devil, monster) in the midst who has to be conquered, dramas on the sports fields and in the chapel (a devil in the chapel) and interpersonal conflicts. Students have been very resourceful: they have used many different locations in the school and included teachers, support staff and children as actors. A selection of images from a lengthy, complex photo-roman *'Trapped'*, made by three boys, is shown in Figures 6.1–6.8. This story is about a monster who appears in the school to terrorise one boy. He then enlists the help of a friend to attack the monster. In this sequence, the boys encounter the monster in the school toilets.

The photo-roman project is considered to be highly successful, especially for the boys. Northmore says:

> The students seem to love it . . . Being the head of school, I don't have as much presence in class as other teachers have, so the children are very independent doing it. The use of the school as the first premise, as metaphor, works well. They can wander around the school making it. They organise it themselves, they are very creative. They recruit others – teachers, other students and support staff – to the cause of being in their films. In 3 years we have had no negative incident.

Boys appear to respond to the project more keenly than girls. Northmore puts this down to a 'phobia with technology amongst girls'. He is delighted that the project can meet the boys' interests as there is not much in school which privileges boys, 'who are tactile, live in the moment and are technologically orientated'. Boys are also marginalised through the assessment practices in the national curriculum, which favour girls' learning styles.

In working in their groups, students have tended to be gender specific, although there are always one or two mixed-gender groups. So far, the boys have tended to make violent photo-romans (e.g. defending the school against an intruder), and the girls emotional or 'chicklet' films (e.g. the loneliness of school). He encourages the boys to make 'emotional films' as 'it is harder to tell a story about an emotional issue'. Visually, it is easier to use violence for dramatic effect as evident, for example, in Hollywood films.

*Figures 6.1–6.3* Still slides from photo-roman *Trapped*

*Figures 6.4–6.6* Still slides from photo-roman *Trapped*

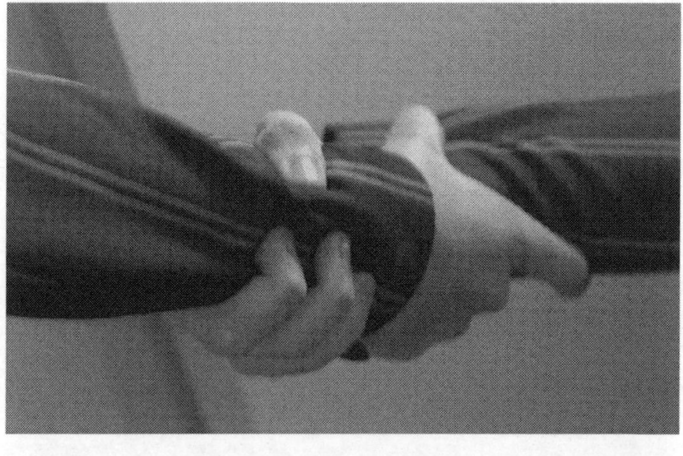

*Figures 6.7–6.8* Still slides from photo-roman *Trapped*

When reflecting on the value of the project and how it could improve, Northmore frames his response in terms of his different identities 'as a principal, an English teacher and an ICT teacher'. He wants to improve the processes of making the films, so students can make better final products. Part of this involves a better integration of the project into a three-year programme, which can develop from Grade 8 through to Grade 10. This is yet to be achieved. From an ICT perspective, students could improve their photo-romans through better, tighter editing: 'We need to do a second round of editing in which they critique each other's products, then go back and make their films tighter. We also need to pay more attention to pace.

They tend to put on the images for too long.' As an English teacher, he sees his focus on 'questions of narrative, how to get more variety in the telling of the stories'. He would like more discussion at the early stages: 'They need to present their stories to the class so we can discuss together what makes a good drama which will engage people's interest.' As a whole class, they need to have a showing and discussion at the rough-cut stage of each photo-roman. This is before they make the final cut. Through this class dialogue between the makers and the class, students can learn a great deal about how to tell visual stories and develop a filmic consciousness. Then, when the project is complete, the plan is that students can organise a special showing 'like the Oscars', where everyone in the school community is invited to come and watch the photo-romans. This raises the stakes for all concerned and attaches a special status to the project.

It is, however, at the level of its potential to develop 'social integration' that Northmore sees its primary value:

> The interesting thing to me is when the group doesn't succeed. I have some failed films. Now when I look at the reasons underlying them it often has more to do with group dynamics than with technical understanding. So it's not that the children don't have the technical skills for example, for taking digital pictures and editing them together into a film . . . it's the lack of cohesion between the group in terms of clearly defining what they want to achieve and then working logically along a series of progressive steps to arrive at that end product that is expected of them and that is immensely interesting to me, more as a principal than as an English teacher.

As he refines the task, Northmore hopes to be able to make interventions at earlier stages in the project which would enable dysfunctional groups to function better.

At the end of the project, all students engaged in a written reflective exercise which focused on group dynamics, technical aspects of making the product and areas for improvement. In answering the question, *What were some of the problems your group experienced making your video this term?* students showed keen awareness of the impact of group dynamics on how the film gets made. A group of boys who made a very successful photo-roman wrote:

> We spent a lot of time arguing about what the monster should look like. James didn't want to act the second part and he was the only other person who could. We struggled to agree on music. We had to redo the story boards because James lost them and James was sometimes bossy e.g. Tree scene.
>
> (Student 1)

> We argued a lot. Some places were too dark to see the shot and they didn't look good with the flash. We also sometimes didn't agree with how the shot should look.
>
> (Student 2)

A group of girls who made a photo-roman on a special birthday at school wrote the following:

> My group only experienced difficulties on getting people and that was it there were no problems otherwise. The rest of the problems were getting props and clothing and some other things. Maybe in my video props will be a problem too because the knives for many people where will I get them. I think our project went well because of group work.
>
> (Student 1)

> The difficulties our group experiences was making an ending of our video that will fit with the story. The editing of the pictures where we had to put in footprints and the hand. Making the story flow from one part to another because we had to take out some of the pictures and thinking of a title. Taking pictures so we didn't have to use too much sound.
>
> (Student 2)

In answering the question, *How did you use the camera angle and type of shot in your photo-roman project this term?* students had to articulate their understandings of the relationship between form and meaning. The boys who made *Trapped* showed a strong technical understanding of filmic techniques and how to write about them:

> We used close-ups to show emotions and extremely long shots to show his absolute desolation and loneliness in the beginning. We also used close-ups to show important actions such as in the scene where boy 1 helps boy 2 in the bathroom. We used a close-up of their hands holding here and when boy 1 finds the stick just before he goes to fight the monster. We also used a very low angle for the picture when boy 1 was hiding in the tree to make him look more safe and powerful. In our movie there are also a lot of action sequences for this we used quite plain medium to long shots but sometimes got higher to show more of the surroundings. The most present thing we used though was sequences such as boy 1 falling off the gate.
>
> (Student 1)

> We used horizontal pictures to show only the object, person or place and we used vertical lines to show a more open picture with lots of

> details behind. When we show our person walking, we used a long shot picture to show head and feet and we kept on going back so it seems the person is walking. When we took a picture of an important object or expression of the face, we used a close-up angle. When our person was walking down the stairs it was kind of a bird's eye view. To show that a person passed an object we close-up angled the object, then showed a long shot of the persons in front of the object.
>
> (Student 2)

When asked, *If you were asked to do the project again, what would you do differently?* students showed a critical awareness of key elements in the genre which could be improved:

> I guess maybe our story because the viewer wouldn't really understand what is happening although you can see what is happening in the beginning. Another think I would change is the environment of the film. We needed different environments but we could only get two out of three. I could also change the clothes we were wearing and make it more not like this school, but a totally different one. The props we had were not very good. That is another thing that I would have changed.
>
> (Student 1)

> Not much. I felt it went really well. Perhaps change the director. Also add a shot of the main character falling asleep and make some shots move faster so it would follow quicker.
>
> (Student 2)

### *The photo-roman project: developing multimodal cohesion*

It is clear from the above account that the photo-roman project operates at multiple levels with different effects and outcomes. My interest is in the use of mode and how this project is extending students' understanding of multimodality. This project is an example of multimodal pedagogy *par excellence* because it is about modes: their forms, their affordances and how they interact in a multimodal ensemble – in this case, the photo-roman – to tell a story. Each photo-roman can be thought of as an identity-text (Cummins 2000, 2005), a complex sign which speaks of the group's interests and knowledges. The project invites students to draw on different kinds of semiotic resources and to distribute expertise among the group. In the first stage, students tell a story only with pictures, without relying on sound or language. This is a major constraint, forcing them to engage with the affordances and limits of still images. Students were conscious of these constraints. One student said, next time she would choose 'an easier story that does not need so much editing and sound effects'. Another student would 'take better pictures to make them more accurate'. Students grappled with how to use the elements of visual composition – colour, light, space, close-ups, long shots, position, perspective – to achieve dramatic effects. In the second stage of the project, students are asked to create a photo-roman using images and sound only. They have to understand the relationship between sound and image, how sound complements image through harmony or rupture. Only in the third stage can students introduce dialogue, the reason being that in many films, dialogue is often superfluous.

Through this task, students are developing an understanding of *multimodal cohesion*: how modes cohere together in multimodal texts and communicative events. Van Leeuwen (2005: 248) conceptualises multimodal cohesion in terms of interactional dynamics and the logic of dialogue, drawing on 'spoken dialogue' and 'musical interaction' for ideas about how modes cohere. Multimodal cohesion is based on *multimodal logic*. The logic of dialogue follows emotional flows within social contexts rather than the logics of 'grammar'. Voloshinov (1986) wrote that 'alternating lines of dialogue':

> Are joined with one another and alternating with one another not according to the laws of grammar or logic, but according to the laws of evaluative (emotive) correspondance, dialogical deployment etc., in close dependence on the historical conditions of the social situation and the whole pragmatic run of life.
>
> (cited in van Leeuwen 2005: 248)

In a multimodal text, like a film, different modes are in dialogue with one another, interacting sequentially and simultaneously. Streams of events may be in harmony or in conflict. Within modes, there is interaction, and between modes there is a dialogue/interaction:

> I will treat semiotic modes as though they are participants in a dialogue, or instruments in an orchestra. I will ask, for instance: Can I understand the interaction between the tracks in a movie – the image track, the dialogue track, the sound effects track(s), the music track – as similar to the interaction between musical instruments playing together? Can I understand the relation between the lyrics and music of a song as a dialogue between two voices which may either agree or disagree?
>
> (van Leeuwen 2005: 249)

In tackling the photo-roman project, students are learning about the potential of semiotic resources, how to use them to design and articulate their meanings. They explore how to use image and sound dialogically for artistic impact. They are making aesthetic choices about the relationship between the images and the music track: should they produce a sense of harmony or discord? At what points should the music complement the image or dominate the image? They are learning that multimodal cohesion involves understanding how the bits hang together within the overall flow of the whole product and how best to combine elements to make the fullest impact on a viewer.

### *Instance of practice 3: hope and the politics of housing: multimodality and multi-perspectivity*

> . . . the politics of housing can be argued to be the single most critical site of a politics of citizenship in this city (Mumbai).
>
> (Appadurai 2002)

Charles Sambo teaches English to Grade 11 students in a co-ed state secondary school in Soweto. The school was built in 1980, four years after the Soweto student uprisings. There is an informal settlement very close to the school where many of the students live. According to Sambo, in spite of living in conditions of suffering and degradation, these students 'perform the best' in class and have 'high hopes' for their futures. Recently, these students have become angry, complaining about how lack of service delivery (sanitation, clean water, electricity) from the government is directly affecting their everyday lives, causing great hardship. They feel marginalised and abandoned in the face of a booming South African economy and a rising black middle class with access to wealth, power and networks which they do not have. They are angry about the inequalities in relation to access to housing: some families appear to be getting government-provided housing and not them. In terms of the housing hierarchy in Johannesburg, it is the poorest people – mostly women and children – who live in these highly populated, degraded and insecure forms of housing with negligible access to essential services. One student described the situation thus:

> Life in shacks is considered a better life than living on the streets but I think it is still the same. They have no water, no electricity and a high risk of fires in shacks. Thousands of people in South Africa die from fire and they are left homeless for days and the government makes promises and never delivers . . .

The students approached their teacher for help in finding appropriate forms of social action to 'voice their complaints'. They wanted to tell people about the difficulties of their lives. Sambo describes the differences between this post-1994 generation and his own, the 1976 generation of student activists:

> This generation was never exposed to the violence that we were exposed to and they don't know about the hardships of the past government . . . they view this government as doing the best for them and they have

> high hopes that they will also be playing a part in their community or society . . . they want to be part of referendums and forums so they can talk about these issues. Sometimes when they complain, their complaints do not reach the targeted groups and they feel abandoned.

Sambo took the decision to focus on inspiring hope:

> My starting point was hope: although there is this turmoil and suffering and lack of being settled, at the end there is hope, and these learners are giving us better results than those learners from the townships . . . it is the learners from the shacks who stay behind for afternoon studies . . . you find that the ones who come from this hardship are the ones who bring better results, there is this thing that drives them, you know, *I am tired of this suffering, I want a better life.*

Working in collaborative partnership, Sambo and the students began the process by producing a workbook on the theme *Shack Life*. The aim of this workbook was to address certain questions: what's a 'shack', what's it like to live in a shack, through what Sambo calls, 'narrations and sentiments echoed by real people with first hand experience'. In producing this workbook, the students aimed to raise community awareness and interest on the topic. The workbook could be read and used as a resource by students and other interested parties. The idea was that it would contain activities and suggestions on how to voice their grievances through research, narratives, letters of complaint, reports and a manifesto for action.

### *What they produced*

Working together for a month, they produced a workbook consisting of the following components:

- a history of informal settlement housing in Soweto written by Sambo;
- official views of the city: maps and tourist postcards of Johannesburg;
- personal narratives of *Shack Life* written by the students;
- poems written and performed by the students;
- a photographic essay on *Shack Life* with photos taken by the students. Figures 6.9–6.12 show a selection of photographs and students' captions from this photographic essay.
- photographs of students performing their poems in class;
- topics for debates and discussion, e.g. the Minister of Housing has said: 'By 2014 we shall have eradicated all the informal settlements . . . everyone will be properly and decently housed.' What do you think about this statement? Discuss your views.
- examples of letters of complaint addressed to local politicians;

*Figure 6.9* Photo essay *Shack Life*. 'The approach to Majazana, meaning "He who sleeps in an overcoat"'

*Figure 6.10* Photo essay *Shack Life*. 'This settlement is close to a valley and there are lots of reeds there. These are the people who suffer the most when it rains a lot because it floods and their houses are taken along'

*Figure 6.11* Photo essay *Shack Life*. 'This family runs a phone business in their yard. The woman was so happy to see us, she called to the young ones, "Come out, you are going to appear in the newspapers . . ."'

*Figure 6.12* Photo essay *Shack Life*. 'Shack dwellers trying to make a living by washing trash bins in the stream. These bins are from the township houses nearby. We use water from this very stream for washing, cooking and drinking'

- example of a report;
- example of manifesto;
- reading, writing and language activities based on all of the above texts.

### *Multimodality and multi-perspectivity*

I find this project interesting as an example of multimodal pedagogy because it brings together, in quite explicit ways, social justice and rights issues with multimodality. Multimodality is affording students the opportunity to represent a range of representations, a multi-perspectival view on the entity 'shack life'. These representations collapse boundaries between 'inside' and 'outside' school spaces. In their absorption and translation of forms of official culture (maps and tourist postcards) with local culture (poetry performances, image-making and activist 'struggle' rhetoric) and school culture (particular forms of reasoning, reading and writing practices) shack life is presented with specificity, through the eyes of its makers.

Here is Thembeka's essay, *Living in a Squatter Camp*:

> Living in a squatter camp is not so healthy but at least I have a roof over my head. It's better than living on the streets with no shelter at all. I live the life of a candle, primus stove and pitch darkness. The paraffin is my perfume and the soot my make-up at home. But nobody can tell right now that I'm from the squatter camp because I'm clean and washed up and in uniform and in school.
>
> Having no electricity does not mean I'm not confident to dream. My confidence is my light at dawn and in the evening.
>
> Although some nights I go to bed on an empty stomach, or eat plain cabbage and porridge, as long as I do not tell, no one will notice. So I can go on living my life with confidence and radiate my love and respect. I come from a decent family though poor. I come from a home. It might be a shack but it's a house of warmth. It might be a shack, but it's also an album of memories. It might be a shack but it's a home full of love.
>
> The midnight candle I burn illuminates my future. I know and believe that education is the key. Where there's a will, there's a way. My school results give me hope. I want to show the world and prove to myself that I can do it. I can achieve my goals! Realize my dreams! I am going to climb those social ladders of success through education and dedication.

And a poem from Pumi:

> A house of corrugated iron
> So small and dark
> Nights under a leaking roof

Stuffy summers
Choking smells
Narrow soiled footpaths
No clean water
Just a small stream
Alongside the settlement

When it rains
Each shack
A bottom-holed boat
No waterborne sewerage
Just small scary
unflushable toilets

Honourable President Mbeki
Started right where I am
I am as proud as him
Of being an African
My A's at school propel me
My peers, my courage
My teachers, my guidance
Myself, strong.

Producing this workbook can be seen as a form of rehearsal. It is an apprenticeship into the steps which need to be taken later (or now) when, as adults, the students might want to produce forms of political consensus which may best advance their interests and those of the community in relation to addressing issues of poverty, wealth, dignity and equality. The conscious use of multimodality frees up the creative space for students to explore a range of different 'voices' in different modalities. Working across boundaries and divisions of knowledge produces *different narrations of 'shack life'* which can speak to a range of audiences and contexts. For example, the photo essay is very evocative in its immediacy. Photographs as forms of evidence, can be used to persuade outsiders to assist in their cause as well as illuminate aspects of life in the settlements which outsiders are oblivious to or deny.

The strength of the workbook lies in the way it sets up official discourses with grassroots views in ironic juxtaposition. This emphasis on insider perspectives, from 'real people who experience it', develops students' capacities and skills in navigating the cultural and social map in which their aspirations are located. Through the focus on forms of deliberation and logic, they can enter and see their situation from multiple perspectives. This develops their abilities to become strategic in their interventions. Hopefully, the practice of these forms of social action within the safety of the school will stand the students in good stead later on.

> It is through the exercise of voice that the sinews of aspiration as a cultural capacity are built and strengthened, and conversely, it is through exercising capacity to aspire that the exercise of voice by the poor will be extended.
>
> (Appadurai 2002: 18)

### *Instance of practice 4: multimodal musicking*

This final example of multimodal pedagogy shows the importance of research into multimodality as a basis for pedagogical and curriculum transformation. The specific instance is the development of learner-centred teaching in South African music education, which, traditionally, has been conceptualised very narrowly in its focus mainly on how to read staff notation.

Susan Harrop-Allin is an ethnomusicologist and music teacher-educator. She is interested in how the music education curriculum can be redesigned to build on children's existing musical practices. Integrating children's everyday knowledges into the learning environment is one of the stated goals of the South African national curriculum (2002) in its efforts to develop more learner-centred classrooms, but teachers have found this very difficult to do in practice (Adler and Reed 2002).

In her work as an ethnomusicologist, Harrop-Allin (2007) researches urban township children's musical games in their free play. Such games, which abound in playgrounds, streets and communities, have been described by Prinsloo (2004) in his work on multimodal children's play in Kwezi Park, Cape Town, and Janks (2007) in her school-based research into township games in an Atteridgeville primary school. Harrop-Allin's focus is on the 'musicking' practices of Soweto boys and girls between the ages of nine and twelve. Small (1998) uses the term 'musicking' to describe many styles of singing, vocalising, chanting, clapping and moving to sounds in dances and in circle, pair and line games. Harrop-Allin has found that children's 'own musical grammar arises prior to and often without musical instruction' and their implicit knowledge of music is usually much more sophisticated than the content they are exposed to in their music education classes (2007: 12).

The children's musical games are richly multimodal and can be quite dazzling in their combination of song, rhythm, dance, gesture, multilingualism and movement. The games range widely in their purposes, functions and meanings. Some are mainly kinetic, involving sounds and the body in either choreographed or improvised dance movements, individually or in group formations. Others involve ironic and witty verbal play on word sounds and their inherent musicality, in other words, their ability to suggest rhythmic and movement patterns. Some musical games have distinctly socialising functions: they develop group cohesion and rule-obeying; they provide a framework for children to explore identities and gender relationships in a safe space; and they develop children's social interaction skills through multiple modes of communication and forms of ritualised play. These games are also platforms for display, providing participants with opportunities to show off their different musical and performance skills.

Usually, these games combine traditional and contemporary urban musical and dance practices. The children draw on semiotic resources within urban culture which are mixes of traditional forms, sources from the media and township style. Some sources are children's 'indigenous' games which have been passed on through school or community. *Two Shelen'*, for example, is adapted from an old Zulu game, expressing personal and family pride. In its traditional form, it is played by girls. The girl in the middle of the ring says her family praise song while everyone around encourages her by responding with *two shelen'*. Part of the art of the game is to fit your praise name into the rhythm of the game. In the contemporary township version of the game, both boys and girls participate. In addition, the genre is looser and more fluid in that not only do children chant their praise names, but add information about their age, where they live and the name of their schools (Harrop-Allin 2007: 18).

*Two shelen'*
(Introduction)

| | |
|---|---|
| Ngake nga hamba wema | (I went for a walk) |
| Nga fika kuleyo ndawo | (I arrived at the place) |
| Bangibuza igama L'ami we ma | (They/the boys asked me my name) |
| Ngathi mina ngingu 'Lindeni' | (My name is Lindeni) |
| Bangibuza igamgalai wema | (They asked me my surname) |

(Individual family praise song)

Ngasho hgathi ngingo wakwa Khumalo we ma (I said my surname is Khumalo)

Unmtungwa umbulazi (That is where the Khumalo's praise song is from)

[The individual carries on from here with her praise song, according to the call and response and rhythmic structure of the game.]

By adopting a multimodal lens through which to view these musical games, Harrop-Allin analyses the complexity of the children's integration of sound, gesture, language, movement, dance and performance in their games. These games give us insight into children's multimodal play outside of formal learning contexts. They are also important sources of information about children's musicking: their use of turn taking, call-and-response, rhythm and dance, clapping and movement. This research provides a basis on which to reconceptualise music education as much more than staff notation. Indeed, it shows clearly the extent to which music education which is taught in an African city, such as Johannesburg, needs to engage with the 'local' and acknowledge the richness of children's embodied musical knowledge, their 'musicking', as a multimodal set of practices which can be drawn upon, developed and extended to produce new musical forms and performance possibilities.

## Concluding remarks

This chapter has focused on instances of classroom practice where teachers have constructed tasks or activities which engage with multimodality. In the same way that there now exists a large body of work which investigates the use and semiotic potential of language in classrooms, we need to develop a body of work which examines, in detailed ways, the different ways in which teachers and learners work with multimodality. This is essential if we wish to develop our understanding of the potential of multimodal pedagogies to improve learning. At the same time, we need to continue to research multimodality in order to see what it has to offer pedagogy and how it can be used for educational change.

In each instance of classroom practice described in this chapter, multimodality has been used to extend and deepen students' relationship to learning. Multimodality, conceptually, offers the opportunity for exploring multiperspectivity, different viewpoints, narrations and translations which constantly change what the object 'is'. In the first example, the teachers are concerned to 'translate' the abstract concepts of the anatomy into more concrete representations. They effect this through a pedagogy of synaesthesia, by asking students to 'translate' their understandings from one mode into another: from drawings into models, from abstract concept into body movement. In the second example, in which students have to create a photo-roman, students have to grapple with what it means to tell a story only through pictures. This task heightens their awareness of the relationship between form and meaning in photographs. In the example of the workbook on *Shack Life*, students began to explore the relationship between rhetoric and mode: for example, that photographs can be used persuasively to present narrative perspectives which letters of complaint as genre cannot do. In all instances, students learn that different modes provide different narratives or 'takes' on the same phenomenon. In the final example, research into the multimodality of children's musical games provides a basis on which to build a new kind of 'multimodal' music education which views children as resourceful, creative and skilled music-makers who have deep knowledge of a musical practice.

Chapter 7

# Representation, rights and resources

In the closing lines of his autobiography, Nelson Mandela wrote:

> When I walked out of prison, that was my mission, to liberate the oppressed and oppressor, both. Some say that has now been achieved. But I know that is not the case. The truth is that we are not yet free: we have merely achieved the freedom to be free, the right not to be oppressed. We have not taken the final step of our journey but the first step on a longer and more difficult road. For to be free is not merely to cast off one's chains, but to live in a way that respects and enhances the freedom of others. The true test of our devotion to freedom is just beginning.
>
> (1994: 617)

*To be free is not merely to cast off one's chains, but to live in a way that respects and enhances the freedom of others.*

I have argued in this book that language and literacy classrooms are potential sites for building democratic culture. Although literacy learning is part of much broader chains of sustainability and development in South Africa, especially in the case of the rural poor (Nelson Mandela Foundation 2005), it is important to focus on the conditions in classrooms which constrain, guide or enable open discussion of different values, perspectives and forms of reasoning. Varenne and McDermott (1998) in their study of successful school failure in American schools, suggest that democracy in classrooms can be thought of in terms of the conditions against which participants struggle that can inhibit or open up possibilities for 'personal action'. Such possibilities for personal action are linked to the extent to which people, together, open up and extend the boundaries of freedom for each other.

The main argument of this book is that the forms of representation through which students are permitted to make their meanings is a critical component in constructing classrooms as hybrid, democratic spaces which value diversity and difference. Positively valuing social difference as a resource is an essential component in building democratic culture, as social difference can encourage a wider range of interactions and perspectives amongst participants (Young 1997; Enslin *et al.* 2001). In this study, I have provided evidence of how a different way of looking at children's meaning-making, through the lens of multimodal social semiotics and elements of ethnography, can reveal the meaning potential in the many cultural sources that children have access to. This meaning potential can be developed for learning in contexts of difference in ways that can contribute to respecting and enhancing students' multiple identities, dignity and senses of self-esteem. In this sense, diversity can be a resource for the practice of freedom.

For historical and political reasons, the examples in this book have focused predominantly on the texts and communicative practices of children from poor or marginalised urban communities in Johannesburg. Although there have been numerous studies of children's meaning-making in the West (e.g. Wells 1987; Dyson 1989, 2003; Fox 1993; Gregory 1997; Gregory and Williams 2000; Bearne 2003; Hall *et al.* 2003; Pahl and Rowsell 2005) the study of children's meaning-making in Africa has received little scholarly attention. This has to do with the invisibility of Africa in dominant Western discourses where Africa is associated with moral and social disintegration, tribalism and the primitive. The value of applying a multimodal perspective to the texts and communicative practices of South African children in this book is that it illuminates their potential and demonstrates the extent to which *all* children's meaning-making is a dynamic, complex and transformative activity in which they actively draw on a multiplicity of semiotic resources which are available to them in their environment, and which they consider apt for their meanings. These semiotic resources are neither static nor fixed: they are socially produced and are part of histories of culturally and historically situated communicative practices which have been developed and transformed through people's ongoing interaction with materiality and the shaping of culture.

Children's meaning-making is a creative practice in which children make conscious and unconscious decisions concerning the design of their texts. They make choices about how to *represent* their meanings, and at the same time, how to *communicate* their meanings to an 'other' – a viewer, a listener, a reader. There are numerous examples in this book of how children actively work with historically established conventions in relation to particular communicative practices, but in doing so, reconfigure and reshape these conventions. These transformations occur in different degrees and at different points in the semiotic process. They are related to the constraints and possibilities of the resources available in the environment, the interests of the individual sign-maker in relation to the communicative context and purpose, and the extent to which the sign-maker has a confidence and 'deep knowledge' of that practice. So, for example, a folkloric animal tale is reshaped as a contemporary political tale with well-known politicians; *Two Shelen*, a game traditionally played by Amazulu girls to show family pride, becomes a mixed-gender urban chant to assert identities; a beaded fertility child figure is refashioned as a doll clothed in folds of bubblewrap; a terrifying cannibal becomes a King Kong figure who eats little girls.

These transformations show the extent to which meaning-making, creativity and innovation are inseparable: every act of representation is a creative act in which a new sign is made. Innovation is the normal condition of all human meaning-making (Kress *et al.* 2001: 8). Exactly how the innovation and creativity is at work in a child's text is not always evident or recognisable at first glance or first reading. For example, I initially assumed that Lungile's version of her grandmother's oral story, *Madevu Mbopha*, recounted in Chapter 3, was an imitation or 'copy' of how her grandmother used to tell it. It was only through a multimodal analysis of the story, which entailed a detailed exploration of all the complex layers in which she was expressing meaning through her voice, her eyes, her smile, her gaze, her hip movements, her arms and her language, that I came to understand the extent to which she was inflecting the text at every level with her own personal, individual style and resources. In this activity, Lungile was creating a new text, a new sign, building on what had come before.

## Becoming good readers of signs

In social semiotic theory, learning and teaching occur through the ongoing creation, reading and mediation of signs within semiotic chains. The activity of teaching and learning involves the use and transformation of multiple semiotic resources – actions, materials, artefacts, technologies – for communication purposes. Teaching and learning as semiotic activity presents new challenges for teachers and for teaching. It means, first, recognising that what goes on in classrooms is forms of sign-making. If it is assumed that teachers and students, together, in joint activity, produce multiple signs, it becomes important for teachers to develop the ability to become 'good readers of signs'. Attending to the full ensemble of communicative modes that are involved in classroom communication can provide a rich perspective on students' learning. Although signs are always only partial representations of the object which is being represented, students' texts, as signs, have to be seen as multimodal to acquire their full meaning (Millard 2006).

What this means, in practice, is that teachers need to systematically attend to how students engage with multimodality in their learning. This means knowing how to help students to become more effective in their use of modes. An important place to begin is to develop the skills of describing the features of children's multimodal texts, for example, knowing how to describe how a child is working with sound, image and narrative to produce a photo-roman, or knowing how features like typography, colour, spatiality and page design contribute to the overall meaning of a student's text. Good teaching and learning materials written for teachers can enable teachers to apply a multimodal social semiotic approach to examining students' texts. The UKLA/QCA (2004/2005) booklets produced for teachers in the UK on multimodality are examples of excellent resources for helping teachers to work with the existing assessment frameworks which can be applied to describing children's multimodal texts. Producing teaching materials like this, which are based on examples of local texts, can demonstrate how students use and transform cultural resources in their meaning-making. Such materials can be of great value to teachers working in diverse cultural and geographical contexts.

Although there are multiple factors at work in the translation and enactment of national curriculum policy into practice, teachers play a central role in the realisation of their subject in their own classrooms. As intellectuals and thinkers, teachers have choices in how to construct their identities as educators (Cummins 2005). They also have choices in how to reframe or imagine alternative ways of 'being' and 'acting' in their classrooms. This book has described instances of teachers who took decisions to re-imagine new ways of working with their students, creating powerful forms of learning. Recognising what students make and do as signs of learning involves a shift in orientation, a different kind of 'reading' and 'looking'. Signs of learning may not be easy to detect or decipher at first, but on close scrutiny, each sign has the potential to reveal 'a world in a grain of sand'. Some worlds may be realised mainly through language. Others may be realised in complex multimodal ensembles which move beyond language, for example, into gestures, action, images or sound. Some may be represented in the absence of language and the presence of silence. The riches in children's texts lie undetected because most teachers need the tools to unearth them.

Developing teachers' knowledge on how to work productively and creatively with multimodality in the classroom is an essential part of teacher education programmes. Visual communication should become central to teacher education curricula across all disciplines. Visual texts include photographs, drawings, illustrations, art images, posters, CD-ROMS, DVDs, cartoons, animations, mind maps, maps, tables and diagrams. In the same way that teachers learn to apply specific text-based interpretive skills to thinking about how language constructs meaning in classroom texts, so teachers need exposure to different methodologies for analysing how visual texts work to produce meaning.

## Multimodality and forms of knowledge

This study has explored the relationship between modes of communication and forms of knowledge. Different modes, in multimodal combinations, realise knowledge in different ways. For example, in Chapter 3, Lungile produces a story in performance, then transforms it into written language and into image. Each text she makes is a new sign, and each sign represents different points of salience or different 'takes' on the same narrative. Each sign produces a new meaning. When all her 'signs' are considered together, as a composite whole, the ensemble produces a multi-perspectival view of the story and the characters. The same may be said for the spoken, written and photographic texts produced in the *Shack Life* workbook, and the Olifantsvlei 'Fresh Stories' Project, in which the use of different modes produced different relations to the narrative and different narratives of identity in the semiotic chain. This multi-perspectivity is clearly evident in *Shack Life*, where the combinations of narrative on shack life from different students produce, to use Young's (1997) term,' a collective social wisdom' which is not available from any one position.

The relationship between modes of communication and knowledge has implications for learning and teaching. Different modes of communication communicate different messages. Language represents knowledge differently to image. As Lemke points out, when we put texts and images together, 'their very incommensurability, the fact that they cannot present exactly the same message, casts doubt on the monological pretensions of either, but particularly those of language' (2002: 322). In the context of mainstream schooling, the only texts which have value, in assessment terms, are the written texts. When one considers the composite body of multi-semiotic textual objects which Lungile, for example, produced on the same subject, it seems untenable that written language occupies the exclusive position of being the only mode of representation which really counts. In South Africa, the requirement of writing in standard English acts as a formidable gate-keeper to schooling success for the majority of South African children.

## Multimodality and assessment practices

There is little doubt that current assessment criteria and practices need to be rethought in the context of 'the multimodal turn'. There is a glaring disjuncture between multimodal pedagogy, multimodal learning and a primarily written assessment process. Although written and oral assessment has been the subject of intense scrutiny over decades, developing assessment tools which take into account the complex inter-relationship of modes in a multimodal text is only beginning. Without reliable assessment tools, multimodal instructional practices carry little weight and authority where it really matters.

What does multimodal assessment look like? Kress *et al.* (2001) point to a key conceptual shift which needs to occur in order to engage seriously with multimodal assessment:

> Given that there is trade across modes, and given that the shape of knowledge is transformed in the shift from one mode to another, there is another vast problem here: the teacher or assessment authority may

> have a specific shape of the knowledge in mind for that particular aspect of the curriculum. In its transduction from one mode into another, say from image to writing, that shape changes. That shift, and the principles of transformation guiding it, may not be overtly recognized by the assessor. Assessment criteria, in other words, may be *mode specific*, while the common-sense assumption is that they are *content specific*
>
> (Kress *et al.* 2001: 176)

In their example from the science classroom, they demonstrate how much of science teaching nowadays proceeds via the use of image – but teachers tend not to assess image in the same way as they do writing. In many English classrooms, where texts are made up of different combinations of modes – words, still and moving images, gestures, sound effects, music and language – teachers focus mainly on the linguistic aspects of texts, often ignoring all the other components which constitute meaning. The development of multimodal assessment tools requires on the one level, a sound understanding of how different modes work individually to produce meaning, and then, how modes work together to produce multimodal cohesion. Deepening our understanding of what modes are and can do – their affordances – is a critical area for further research.

Newfield *et al.* (2003) describe the complexity of developing a multimodal assessment tool to measure an artifact produced by a class of Soweto high-school students who, as a group, produced a 'multimodal identity text', the handmade TEBUWA cloth. The cloth as an artwork containing visual, verbal and three-dimensional artifacts, was composed of individually-written poems, as well as collaboratively-produced elements such a multiple layers of stitching and embroidery. The authors argue that new criteria need to be developed which address the fact of multimodality: what multimodality is, and what it does to achieve its effects. In many examples of multimodal texts, like the TEBUWA cloth, the individual voices have less value in themselves, but are meaningful in terms of their function with respect to the whole. In discussing the assessment of the TEBUWA cloth, Newfield *et al.* state they were interested in:

> The assessment of the cloth as product and process that speaks to the complex orchestration of its voices and modes, to evidence of its learning and creativity, in a sensitive and flexible way, that is able to celebrate the profundity of its achievement.
>
> (2003: 73)

Drawing on assessment practices in art education, which emphasise the relationship between process and reflection, they included a more participatory, ethnographic-style dimension to the assessment process where discussions with students took place on their interpretations of how they could make different modes work for them, in order to realise their projected interests through the overall design. The authors suggest that assessment should explore the idea of 'resourcefulness' as an overarching category. Resourcefulness would signal the learner's engagement in relation to his or her 'representational resources' and would include the extent to which students are able to recruit 'apt' resources for making their meaning and their ability to use them generatively and productively with evidence of linkages and cohesion across modes and genres.

In relation to assessing students' multimodal online texts, Wyatt-Smith and Kimber (2005) draw on research from a five-year Australian national study (2003–2007) of first- and third-year high-school students, examining how well students research existing knowledge and use it to create and represent new knowledge in the form of online multimodal texts. Arguing that traditional theoretical and policy frameworks for literacy and assessment are orientated towards reading and print and do not readily transfer to technology-mediated literacies as actually practised, Wyatt-Smith and Kimber pose the question: What are relevant and useful assessment criteria to inform teachers' and students' efforts at talking about and determining quality in students' multimodal online texts? The authors work closely with the idea of giving students agency and developing their critical literacy to develop a set of criteria, namely e-proficiency, cohesion, content and design. These criteria can be used to identify and talk about the elements of multimodal texts, focusing on the component parts of the text, with each criterion given separate consideration. In addition to this, they develop a category, 'transmodality', in order to examine the text more holistically. Transmodality captures the essence of working within and across modes, as well as the 'synergistic dynamics' of text production online. They claim that a focus on transmodal operation, in conjunction with explicitly defined assessment criteria, allows a more concentrated focus on human agency in designing.

In an analysis of the shifts since the 1990s in what constitutes 'text' in the Advanced Level English Language examination papers in the United Kingdom, Shortis and Jewitt (2005) explore the changes in the construction of subject English and its assessment. Before 2000, the texts used for analysis were re-set in a word processed format which stripped them of their original materiality and design including their use of image, font, layout and colour. Since 2001, the texts have been consistently reproduced in facsimile form in a state of 'ecological materiality' in which the linguistic is set alongside and within other signifiers: these include the original graphology, use of image and layout. Although the questions set on the text still require students to pay attention mainly to the linguistic features, there is some focus on the multimodal features of the text. By according value to everyday texts such as postcards, emails and handwritten notes, for example, and by loosening the boundaries between the visual and the linguistic in textual practice, the 'picket fence demarcations' around the sub-Englishes of English Language,

Communication and Media Studies, are challenged. The authors argue that these changes to how texts are represented in examination contexts point to small shifts in thinking about what constitutes text, textual practices and textual responses in the English classroom: that 'text is made in artifacts and not made exclusively by language', and 'by always showing layout, the linguistic becomes embedded within a multimodal semiotic' (2005: 86–8). Ferreira (2006) complements this work by showing how spaces for multiliteracies and multimodality can be 'prised open' in standardised examinations, citing examples of political cartoons, advertisements and postcards from the national school-leaving English Language examination in South Africa. As Chief Examiner, she argues that it is not enough to simply select multimodal texts: much hinges on the types of questions which are posed about these texts. Ferreira claims that standardised tests can be enhanced by a multiliteracies pedagogy, and in so doing can encourage innovation and change.

## Multimodality and bodily practices

Modes are produced in and by the body. The body articulates meaning. There are numerous instances in this research of how children have used their bodies as multimodal signs and resources for meaning. For example, Lungile's storytelling performances are all body, inscribed with culturally specific ways of moving, talking, gesturing, seeing and interacting with an audience. The Olifantsvlei children used their bodies to make, see, feel, touch, smell, move and hold their doll/child figures: indeed, it was in the sensory act of holding the dolls that new ideas were imagined. The children who made images of cannibal figures were drawing on rich visual repertoires in representing their feelings and fears. In children's musical games, they use multimodal combinations of sound, movement, language, clapping and rhythm to negotiate relationships and identities. The examples in this book point to the notion of an integrated relation, rather than a separation, between thought, imagination, affectivity and the senses. Bodies hold history, memory, thought, feelings and desires. Bodies hold language and silence. Our bodies are repositories of knowledge, but these knowledges are not always knowable in and through language – they can be felt, imagined, imaged or dreamed.

This notion of the body as both repository and resource for the expression of different knowledges, feelings, sensual memories and thoughts points to the possibility of imagining teaching and learning as a whole-body practice. This implies the need for more heightened awareness in classroom communities of the different ways in which participants engage with representational forms, displaying culturally specific relationships to culture, history and identity *through their bodies.* Teachers can become more aware of how children use their bodies in diverse, culturally and gendered inflected ways, and how these bodily differences can be used as a productive resource for the exploration of cultural and social difference. When learners use their senses in making and touching objects, tracing shapes, responding to and creating images and sounds, they draw on particular histories of relationships to these senses. In reading the body as a multimodal sign, teachers and learners become involved in textual practices in which not only the sign itself, but the conditions of embodiment of the sign-maker form part of how multi-semiotic texts are to be created, interpreted and valued.

## Multimodality, representation, rights and resources

South Africa is emerging from a long history of violence, brutality and racism. In an attempt to build a more just, humane society, it is critical to focus attention on the rights, needs and dignity of children, who were the most vulnerable in relation to the atrocities of apartheid, and are the most affected by conditions of poverty. These rights include the right to learn. But what is the meaning of the 'right to learn' if who you are and what you know, in other words, your resources for representing your meanings, have no value for those who hold power in classroom spaces? In this book, I have argued against notions of singularity and narrowness: rather, I have tried to show that classroom cultures which actively encourage open discussion and multiple forms of perspectivity in which different knowledges and cultural forms are 'remixed' and rubbed up against each other can create more just learning environments, and also lead to new forms, new meanings and new possibilities for learning. The concept of multimodality, and its multiple applications to pedagogy, is an important starting point for such a project.

# Bibliography


Abraham, S.Z. (2001) 'Abduction', unpublished paper, University of the Witwatersrand.

Adler, J. and Reed, Y. (eds) (2002) *Challenges of Teacher Development: an Investigation of Take-up in South Africa*, Pretoria: Van Schaik.

AIDS Foundation, SA (2005) 'HIV/AIDS in South Africa', www.aids.org.za/hiv.htm (accessed April 10, 2007).

Anzaldua, G. (ed.) (1990) *Making Face, Making Soul/Haciendo Caras: Creative and Critical Perspectives by Feminists of Colour*, San Francisco, CA: Aunt Lute.

Appadurai, A. (2002) 'The capacity to aspire: culture and the terms of recognition', paper presented at Wits Institute for Social and Economic Research (WISER) Seminar, University of the Witwatersrand, Johannesburg, South Africa, 29 August.

Archer, A. (2006) 'Opening up spaces through symbolic objects: harnessing students' multimodal resources in developing English academic literacy in an Engineering course', *English Studies in Africa* 49 (1): 189–206.

Austin, J. L. (1962) *How to do Things with Words*, Cambridge, MA: Harvard University Press.

Baker, D. and Street, B. (2006) 'So, What About Multimodal Literacies?' in K. Pahl and J. Rowsell (eds) *Travel Notes from the New Literacy Studies*, Clevedon: Multilingual Matters.

Baker, D., Clay, J. and Fox, C. (eds) (1996) *Challenging Ways of Knowing in English, Mathematics and Science*, London: Falmer Press.

Bakhtin, M. (1981) *The Dialogic Imagination*, Austin, TX: University of Texas Press.

Bakhtin, M. (1986) *Speech Genres and Other Late Essays*, Austin, TX: University of Texas Press.

Barber, K. (ed) (1997) *Readings in African Popular Culture*, London: James Currey.

Barnes, D. (1976) *From Communication to Curriculum*, Harmondsworth: Penguin.

Barthes, R. (1973) *Mythologies*, London: Paladin.

Bartlett, L. and Holland, D. (2002) 'Theorising the space of literacy practices', *Ways of Knowing Journal* 2 (1) 10–22.

Barton, D. (1994) *Literacy: an Introduction to the Ecology of Written Language*, Oxford: Blackwell.

Barton, D. and Hamilton, M. (1998) *Local Literacies*, London and New York: Routledge.

Barton, D., Hamilton, M. and Ivanic, R. (eds) (2000) *Situated Literacies: Reading and Writing in Context*, London and New York: Routledge.

Bauman, R. (1986) *Story, Performance and Event: Contextual Studies of Oral Narrative*, Cambridge: Cambridge University Press.

Baynham, M. (1995) *Literacy Practices: Investigating Literacy in Social Contexts*, London: Longman.

Baynham, M. and Baker, D. (2002) "Practice" in literacy and numeracy research: multiple perspectives', *Ways of Knowing Journal* 2 (1): 1–9.

Bearne, E. (2003) 'Rethinking literacy: communication, representation and text', *Reading: Literacy and Language* 37 (3): 98–103.

Behar, R. (1994) *Translated Women: Crossing the Border with Esperanza's Story*, Boston, MA: Beacon.

Berger, J. (1972) *Ways of Seeing*, Harmondsworth: Penguin.

Bernstein, B. (1990) *The Structure of Pedagogic Discourse: Class, Codes and Control, Vol. IV*, London: Routledge.

Bhattacharya, R., Gupta, S., Jewitt, C. Newfield, D. Reed, Y. and Stein, P. (2007) 'The policy-practice nexus in English classrooms in Delhi, Johannesburg and London: teachers and the textual cycle', *TESOL Quarterly* 41 (3).

Birdwhistell, R. L. (1970) *Kinesics and Context: Essays in Body Motion Communication*, Philadelphia, PA: University of Pennsylvania Press.

Bloch, C. and Alexander, N. (2003) 'Aluta Continua: the Relevance of the Continua of Biliteracy to South African Multilingual Schools', in N. Hornberger (ed.) *Continua of Biliteracy: an Ecological Framework for Educational Policy, Research and Practice in Multilingual Settings*, Clevedon: Multilingual Matters.

Bloch, C., Stein, P. and Prinsloo, M. (2001) 'Progress report on children's early literacy learning (CELL) research project in South Africa', *Journal of Early Childhood Literacy* 1 (1) :121–2.

Bourdieu, P. (1990) *The Logic of Practice*, (R. Nice, trans.) Cambridge: Polity Press.

Bourdieu, P. (1991) *Language and Symbolic Power*, London: Polity Press.

Brandt, D. and Clinton, K. (2002) 'The limits of the local: expanding perspectives of literacy as a social practice', *Journal of Literacy Research* 34 (3): 337–56.

Brandt, D. and Clinton, K. (2006) 'Afterword', in K. Pahl and J. Rowsell (eds) *Travel Notes from the New Literacy Studies: Instances of Practice*, Clevedon: Multilingual Matters.

Brumfit, C. and Johnson, K. (eds) (1979) *The Communicative Approach to Language Teaching*, Oxford: Oxford University Press.

Bruner, J. (1986) *Actual Minds, Possible Worlds*, Cambridge, MA: Harvard University Press.

Burman, S. and Reynolds, P. (eds) (1986) *Growing Up in a Divided Society: the Contexts of Childhood in South Africa*, Johannesburg: Ravan Press.

Burn, A. and Parker, D. (2003) 'Tiger's Big Plan: Multimodality and the Moving Image', in C. Jewitt and G. Kress (eds) *Multimodal Literacy*, New York: Peter Lang.

Butler, J. (1990) *Gender Trouble: Feminism and the Subversion of Identity*, London: Routledge.

Canagarajah, A. Suresh (ed.) (2005) *Reclaiming the Local in Language Policy and Practice*, Mahwah, NJ: Lawrence Erlbaum Associates.

Cazden, C.B. (1988, 2nd edn 1997) *Classroom Discourse: the Language of Teaching and Learning*, Portsmouth, NH: Heinemann.

Centre for the Study of Violence and Reconciliation (1997) 'Youth, Streetculture and Urban Violence in Africa', Johannesburg: Centre for the Study of Violence and Reconciliation.

Christie, P. (1992) *The Right to Learn: the Struggle for Education in South Africa*, Johannesburg: SACHED/Ravan.

Chubb, K. and Van Dijk, L. (2001) *Between Anger and Hope: South Africa's Youth and the Truth and Reconciliation Commission*, Johannesburg: Witwatersrand University Press.

Collins, P. (1990) *Black Feminist Thought: Knowledge, Consciousness and the Politics of Empowerment*, New York: Routledge, Chapman and Hall.

Collins, T. and Stadler, J. (2001) 'Love, passion and play: sexual meaning among youth in the Northern Province of South Africa', paper presented at AIDS in Context Conference, University of the Witwatersrand, Johannesburg, April.

Comaroff, J. and Comaroff, J. (1987) 'The madman and the migrant', *American Ethnologist* 14 (2): 198–211.

Cope, B. and Kalantzis, M. (2000) *Multiliteracies: Literacy Learning and the Design of Social Futures*, comp. New London Group, London and New York: Routledge.

Coplan, D. (1994) *In the Time of the Cannibals: the Word Music of South Africa's Basotho Migrants*, Chicago, IL and London: The University of Chicago Press.

Cummins, J. (2000), *Language, Power and Pedagogy: Bilingual Children in the Crossfire*, Clevedon: Multilingual Matters.

Cummins, J. (2005) 'Afterword', in K. Pahl and J. Rowsell (eds) *Literacy and Education: Understanding New Literacy Studies in the Classroom*, London: Sage.

Daniels, H. (2001) *Vygotsky and Pedagogy*, New York and London: Routledge.

Das, V. (1996) 'Language and body: transactions in the construction of pain', *Daedulus* 25 (1): 67–92.

Dawes, A. and Donald, D. (eds) (1994) *Childhood and Adversity: Psychological Perspectives from South African Research*, Cape Town: David Philip.

Dell, E. (ed.) (1998) 'Introduction', in E. Dell (ed.) *Evocations of the Child: Fertility Figures of the Southern African Region*, Cape Town: Human and Rousseau; Johannesburg: The Johannesburg Art Gallery.

Dell, E. (2004) 'Umndwana-Ndebele Beaded Child', in A. Nettleton, A.J. Charlton and F. Rankin-Smith (eds) *Voice-Overs: Wits Writings Exploring African Artworks*, Johannesburg: University of the Witwatersrand Art Galleries.

De Certeau, M. (1984) *The Practice of Everyday Life*, trans. S. Rendell, Berkeley CA: University of California Press.

De Klerk, V. (1995) 'Bilingualism, the Devil and the Big, Wide World', in K. Heugh, A. Siegrühn and P. Plüddemann (eds) *Multilingual Education for South Africa*, Johannesburg: Heinemann.

De Klerk, V. (2002) 'Language issues in our schools: whose voice counts? Part 1: The parents speak', *Perspectives in Education* 20 (1): 1–14.

Delius, P. and Glaser, C. (2002) 'Sexual socialisation in South Africa: a historical perspective', *African Studies* 60 (1): 27–54.

Delius, P. and Walker, L. (2002) 'AIDS in context', *African Studies* 61 (1): 5–12.

Denzin, N.K. and Lincoln, Y.S. (2000) 'The discipline and practice of qualitative research', in N.K. Denzin and Y.S. Lincoln (eds) *Handbook of Qualitative Research*, 2nd edn, London: Thousand Oaks; New Delhi: Sage Publications.

Department of Education (1996), *Curriculum Framework for General and Further Education and Training*, Pretoria: Department of Education.

Department of Education (2002) *Revised National Curriculum Statement Grades R-9 (Schools): Policy Overview*, Pretoria: Department of Education.

Diabate, I. (1999) 'Les Gouts', *Revue Noire* 31: 28.

Donald, D., Dawes, D. and Louw, J. (eds) (2000) *Addressing Childhood Adversity*, Cape Town and Johannesburg: David Phillip.

Dyson, A.H. (1989) *Multiple Worlds of Child Writers: Friends Learning to Write*, New York: Teachers College Press.

Dyson, A.H. (2003) *The Brothers and Sisters Learn to Write: Popular Literacies in Childhood and School Cultures*, New York: Teachers College Press.

Enslin, P., Pendlebury, S. and Tjattis, M. (2001) 'Deliberative democracy, diversity and the challenges of citizenship education', *Journal of Philosophy of Education* 35 (1): 115–30.

Fairclough, N. (1989) *Language and Power*, London and New York: Longman.

Farnell, B. (ed.) (1995) *Human Action Signs in Cultural Contexts. The Visible and the Invisible in Movement and Dance*. Metuchen, NJ and London: Scarcrois Press.

Ferreira, A. (2006) 'Multiliteracies and standardised examinations: a personal reflection on the South African matric English language examination', *English Studies in Africa* 49 (1): 163–88.

Finnegan, R. (1992) *Oral Traditions and the Verbal Arts: a Guide to Research Practices*, London and New York: Routledge.

Finnegan, R. (2002) *Communicating: the Multiple Modes of Human Interconnection*. London and New York: Routledge.

Flewitt, R. (2006) 'Using video to investigate preschool classroom interaction: education research assumptions and methodological practices', *Visual Communication* 5 (1) 25–50.

Foucault, M. (1979) *Discipline and Punish: the Birth of the Prison*, trans. A. Sheridan, London: Peregrine.

Fox, C. (1993) *At the Very Edge of the Forest*, London: Cassell.

Franks, A. (1996) 'Drama education, the body and representation (or, the mystery of the missing bodies)', *Research in Drama Education* 1 (1): 105–20.

Freebody, P. and Freiberg, J. (2007) 'Globalised Literacy Education: Intercultural Trade in Textual and Cultural Practice', in M. Prinsloo and M. Baynham (eds) *Theory and Research in the New Literacy Studies*, Amsterdam: John Benjamins.

Freire, P. (1970) *Pedagogy of the Oppressed*, New York: Seabury Press.

Freire, P. and Macedo, D. (1987) *Literacy: Reading the Word and Reading the World*, Hadley, MA: Bergin and Garvey.

Furniss, G. and Gunner, L. (eds) (1995) *Power, Marginality and African Oral Literature*, Cambridge University Press: Cambridge.

Gardner, H. (1993) *The Unschooled Mind*, London: Fontana Press.

Gee, J.P. (1992) *The Social Mind: Language, Ideology and Social Practice*, London: Bergin & Gravey.

Gee, J.P. (1996) *Social Linguistics and Literacies: Ideology in Discourses*, 2nd edn, London: Falmer Press.

Gee, J.P. (2003) *What Video Games Have to Teach Us about Learning and Literacy*, New York: Palgrave Macmillan.

Gee, J.P. (2004) 'Language in the Science Classroom: Academic Social Languages as the Heart of School-based Literacy', in E. Wendy Saul (ed.) *Crossing Borders in Literacy and Science Instruction: Perspectives on Theory and Practice*, Neward, DE: International Reading Association; Arlington, VA: National Science Teachers Associated Press.

Geertz, C. (1973) *The Interpretation of Cultures: Selected Essays*, New York: Basic Books.

Geertz, C. (1983) *Local Knowledge: Further Essays in Interpretive Anthropology*, New York: Basic Books.

Gibson, J.J. (1979) *The Ecological Approach to Visual Perception*, Boston, MA: Houghton Mifflin.

Giddens, A. (1991) *Modernity and Self-identity: Self and Society in the Late Modern Age*, Cambridge: Polity Press.

Gillen, J. and Hall, N. (2003) 'The Emergence of Early Childhood Literacy', in N. Hall, J. Larson and J. Marsh (eds) *Handbook of Early Childhood Literacy*, London: Thousand Oaks; New Delhi: Sage Publications.

Giroux, H. (1992) *Border Crossings: Cultural Workers and the Politics of Education*, New York: Routledge.

Goodwyn, A. (2005) 'Editorial', *English in Education* 39 (2): 1–4.

Granville, S., Janks, H., Mphahlele, M., Reed, Y. and Watson, P. (1998) 'English with or without g(u)ilt: a position paper on language-in-education policy for South Africa', *Language and Education* 12 (4): 254–72.

Gregory, E. (ed.) (1997) *One Child, Many Worlds: Early Learning in Multicultural Communities*, London: David Fulton.

Gregory, E. and Williams, A. (2000) *City Literacies: Learning to Read Across Generations and Across Cultures*, London: Routledge.

Gunner, L. (2004) 'Africa and Orality', in A. Irele and S. Gikandi (eds) *Cambridge History of African and Caribbean Literature*, vol. I, Cambridge: Cambridge University Press.

Gunner, L. (2006) 'Zulu Choral Music Performing Identities in a New State', *Research in African Literatures* 37 (2): 83–97.

Haffejee, S. (2006) 'Waiting Opportunities: Adolescent girls experiences of gender-based violence at schools', www.csvr.org.za/papers/paphaff-htm (accessed Feb. 16, 2007)

Hall, H., Larson, J. and Marsh, J. (eds) (2003) *Handbook of Early Childhood Literacy*, London: Thousand Oaks; New Delhi: Sage Publications.

Halliday, M.A.K. (1978) *Language as a Social Semiotic: the Social Interpretation of Language and Meaning*, London: Edward Arnold.

Halliday, M.A.K. (1985) *An Introduction to Functional Grammar*, London: Edward Arnold.

Halliday, M.A.K. (1989) *Spoken and Written Language*, Oxford: Oxford University Press.

Hamilton, C. (1998) 'Women and Material Markers of Identity', in E. Dell (ed.) *Evocations of the Child: Fertility Figures of the Southern African Region*, Cape Town: Human and Rousseau and Johannesburg: The Johannesburg Art Gallery.

Harber, K. (1998) 'Venda and Pedi', in E. Dell (ed.) *Evocations of the Child: Fertility Figures of the Southern African Region*, Cape Town: Human and Rousseau and Johannesburg: The Johannesburg Art Gallery.

Harmer, J. (1983) *The Practice of English Language Teaching*, London and New York: Longman.

Harrop-Allin, S. (2007) 'Recruiting learners musical games as resources for South African primary school arts and culture education using a multiliteracies approach', unpublished Masters research report, University of the Witwatersrand.

Hartshorne, K. (1992) *Crisis and Challenge, Black Education 1910–1990*, Cape Town: Oxford University Press.

Heath, S.B. (1983) *Ways with Words: Language, Life and Work in Communities and Classrooms*, Cambridge: Cambridge University Press.

Henderson, P. (1999) 'Living with fragility: children in New Crossroads', unpublished thesis, University of Cape Town.

Heugh, K. (2002) 'The case against bilingual and multilingual education in South Africa: laying bare the myths', *Perspectives in Education* 20 (1):171–96.

Heugh, K., Siegrühn, A. and Plüddemann, P. (eds) (1995) *Multilingual Education for South Africa*, Johannesburg: Heinenmann.

Hobsbawm, E. and Ranger, T. (1984) *The Invention of Tradition*, Cambridge: Cambridge University Press.

Hodge, R. and Kress, G. (1988) *Social Semiotics*, Cambridge: Polity Press.

Hofmeyr, I. (1994) *'We Spend our Years as a Tale that is Told': Oral Historical Narrative in a South African Chiefdom*, Portsmouth, NH: Heinemann; Johannesburg: Witwatersrand University Press; London: James Currey.

Hofmeyr, I. (2004) *The Portable Bunyan*, Johannesburg: Wits University Press.

Hofstadter, D. (1985) *Metamagical Themas: Questing for the Essence of Mind and Pattern*, London and New York: Penguin.

hooks, b. (1990) *Yearning: Race, Gender and Cultural Politics*, Boston, MA: South End.

Hymes, D. (ed.) (1996) *Ethnography, Linguistics, Narrative Inequality: Towards an Understanding of Voice*, London: Routledge.

Iedema, R. (2003) 'Multimodality, resemiotization: extending the analysis of discourse as multi-semiotic practice', *Visual Communication* 2 (1): 29–57.

Jacobs, J.U. (1992) 'Narrating the Island: Robben Island in South African literature', *Current Writing* 4 (1): 73–84.

Jacobsen, G.P. (2002) 'Our great and noble profession', *American Journal of Audiology* (11): 54–5.

James, D. (1999) *Songs of the Women Migrants: Performance and Identity in South Africa*, London: University of Edinburgh Press.

Janks, H. (2000) 'Domination, access, diversity, design: a synthesis for critical literacy education', *Educational Review* 52 (2): 175–86.

Janks, H. (2006) 'Games Go Abroad', *English Studies in Africa* 49 (1): 115–38.

Janks, H. and Comber, B. (2006) 'Critical Literacy Across Continents', in K. Pahl and J. Rowsell (eds) *Travel Notes from the New Literacy Studies: Instances of Practice*, Clevedon: Multilingual Matters.

Jaworksi, A. and Sachdev, I. (1998) 'Beliefs about silence in the classroom', *Language in Education* 12 (4): 273–92.

Jewitt, C. (2002) 'The move from page to screen: the multimodal shaping of school English', *Visual Communication* 1 (2): 171–95.

Jewitt, C. (2005) 'Classrooms and the design of pedagogic discourse: a multimodal approach', *Culture and Psychology* 11 (3): 309–20.

Jewitt, C. (2006) *Technology, Literacy, Learning: a Multimodal Approach*, London: Routledge-Falmer.

Jewitt, C. (2008) 'Multi-modal Discourse Across the Curriculum', in N. Hornberger (ed.) *Encyclopedia of Language and Education*, 2nd revd edn, New York: Springer-Verlag.

Jewitt, C. and Kress, G. (eds) (2003) *Multimodal Literacy*, New York: Peter Lang.

Jewkes, R. (2001) 'Gender-based violence, gender inequalities and the HIV epidemic', paper presented at the AIDS in Context Conference, University of the Witwatersrand, Johannesburg, April.

Jewkes, R., Levin, J., Bradshaw, D. and Mbananga, N. (2002) 'Rape of girls in South Africa', *The Lancet* 359: 319–20.

Johnson, L. and Budlender, D. (2002) *HIV Risk Factors: A Review of the Demographic, Socio-economic, Biomedical and Behavioural Determinants of HIV Prevalence in South Africa*, Cape Town: Centre for Actuarial Research (CARE), University of Cape Town.

Jones, S. (1993) *Assaulting Childhood: Children's Experiences of Migrancy and Hostel Life in South Africa*, Johannesburg: Witwatersrand University Press.

Kallaway, P. (1984) (ed.) *Apartheid and Education*, Johannesburg: Ravan Press.

Kendrick, M., Jones, S., Mutonyi, H. and Norton, B. (2006) 'Multimodality and English education in Ugandan schools', *English Studies in Africa* 49 (1): 95–114.

Kenner, C. (2004) *Becoming Literate: Young Children Learning Different Writing Systems*, Stoke on Trent: Trentham Books.

Knutsson, K.E. and O'Dea, P. (1998) *Children's Rights and Development in South Africa*, Pretoria, South Africa: UNICEF.

Kress, G. (1993) 'Against arbitrariness: the social production of the sign as a foundational issue in critical discourse analysis', *Discourse and Society* 4 (2): 169–93.

Kress, G. (1994) *Learning to Write*, 2nd edn, London: Routledge.

Kress, G. (1995) *Writing the Future: English and the Making of a Culture of Innovation*, Sheffield: National Association for the Teaching of English.

Kress, G. (1997a) *Before Writing: Rethinking the Paths to Literacy*, London and New York: Routledge.

Kress, G. (1997b) 'Multimodal texts and critical discourse analysis', unpublished paper, Institute of Education, University of London.

Kress, G. (2000a) 'Multimodality', in B. Cope and M. Kalantzis (eds), *Multiliteracies: Literacy Learning and the Design of Social Futures*, comp. New London Group, London and New York: Routledge.

Kress, G. (2000b) 'Design and Transformation: New Theories of Meaning', in B. Cope and M. Kalantzis (eds) *Multiliteracies: Literacy Learning and the Design of Social Futures*, comp. New London Group, London and New York: Routledge.

Kress, G. (2003) *Literacy in the New Media Age*, London and New York: Routledge.

Kress, G. and van Leeuwen, T. (1996; 2nd edn 2006) *Reading Images: the Grammar of Visual Design*, London: Routledge.

Kress, G. and van Leeuwen, T. (2001) *Multimodal Discourse: the Modes and Media of Contemporary Communication*, London: Edward Arnold.

Kress, G. and van Leeuwen, T. (2002) 'Colour as a semiotic mode: notes for a grammar of colour', *Visual Communication* 1 (3): 343–68.

Kress, G., Jewitt, C., Ogborn, J. and Tsatsarelis, C. (2001) *Multimodal Teaching and Learning: the Rhetorics of the Science Classroom*, London: Continuum.

Kress, G., Jewitt, C., Bourne, J., Franks, A., Hardcastle, J., Jones, K. and Reid, E. (2005) *English in Urban Classrooms: a Multimodal Perspective on Teaching and Learning*, London: RoutledgeFalmer.

Lancaster, L. (2001) 'Staring at the page: the functions of gaze in a young child's interpretation of symbolic forms', *Journal of Early Childhood Literacy*, 1 (2): 131–52.

Lave, J. and Wenger, E. (1991) *Situated Learning: Legitimate Peripheral Participation*, Cambridge: Cambridge University Press.

Leatt, A. (2006) 'Child Poverty: its Meaning and Extent', in J. Movson, K. Hall, C. Smith and M. Shung-King (eds) *South Africa Child Gauge 2006*, Rondebosch: Children's Institute, University of Cape Town.

Lemke, J. (2000) 'Introduction: language and other semiotic systems in education', *Linguistics and Education* 10 (3): 307–34.

Lemke, J. (2002) 'Travels in hypermodality', *Visual Communication* 1 (3): 299–325.

LoveLife (2001) *Looking at* LoveLife: *the First Year*, Johannesburg: LoveLife.

Luke, A. (1992) 'The body literate: discourse and inscription in early literacy training', *Linguistics and Education* 4 (1): 107–29.

Luke, A. (2004) 'Two Takes on the Critical', in B. Norton and K. Tooney (eds) *Critical Pedagogies and Language Learning*, Cambridge: Cambridge University Press.

Luke, A. (2005) 'Foreword', in K. Pahl and J. Rowsell (eds) *Literacy and Education: Understanding the New Literacy Studies in the Classroom*, London: Sage.

Macdonald, C. (1990) *Crossing the Threshold into Standard Three in Black Education*, Consolidated Main Report of the Threshold Project, Human Sciences Research Council, Pretoria, South Africa.

Mclaren P. (1989) *Life in Schools: an Introduction to Critical Pedagogy in the Foundations of Education*, White Plains, NY: Longman.

Malaquais, D. (2006) 'Quelle Liberte: Art, Beauty and the Grammars of Resistance in Douala', in S. Nuttall (ed.) *Beautiful Ugly: Africa and Diaspora Aesthetics*, Durham and London: Duke University Press.

Mandela, N. (1994) *Long Walk to Freedom: the Autobiography of Nelson Mandela*, Randburg, South Africa: Macdonald Purnell.

Martinec, R. (2000) 'Construction of identity in Michael Jackson's *Jam*', *Social Semiotics* 10 (3): 313–29.

Mauthner, M. (1997) 'Methodological aspects of collecting data from children: lessons from three research projects', *Children and Society* 11 (1): 16 -28.

Mbembe, A. (2001) *On the Postcolony*, Berkeley and Los Angeles, CA: University of California Press.

Mbembe, A. (2002) 'Translation and tradition', paper delivered at Interface: International Symposium on Art and Culture, Wits Institute for Social and Economic Research (WISER) and Wits School of Arts, University of the Witwatersrand, Johannesburg, South Africa, 22 March.

Mbembe, A. (2006) 'Variations on the Beautiful in Congolese Worlds of Sound', in S. Nuttall (ed.) *Beautiful Ugly: African and Diaspora Aesthetics*, Durham and London: Duke University Press.

Menezes de Souza L.M.T. (2005) 'The Ecology of Writing among the Kashinawa: Indigenous Multimodality in Brazil', in A. Suresh Canagarajah (ed.) *Reclaiming the Local in Language Policy and Practice*, Mahwah, NJ: Lawrence Erlbaum Associates.

Millard, E. (2006) 'Transformative Pedagogy: Teachers Creating a Literacy of Fusion', in K. Pahl and J. Rowsell (eds) *Travel Notes from the New Literacy Studies: Instances of Practice*, Clevedon: Multilingual Matters.

Mofolo, T. (1981) *Chaka*, trans. D. Kunene, London: Heinemann.

Mohlala, F. (2001) Untitled paper, University of the Witwatersrand.

Morson, J., Hall, K., Smith, C. and Shung-King, M. (2006) (eds) *South African Child Gauge 2006*, Rondebosch: Children's Institute, University of Cape Town.

Nel, K. and Leibhammer, N. (1998) 'Evocations of the Child', in E. Dell (ed.) *Evocations of the Child: Fertility Figures of the Southern African Region*, Cape Town: Human and Rousseau and Johannesburg: The Johannesburg Art Gallery.

Nelson Mandela Foundation/HSRC (2005) *Emerging Voices: a Report on Education in South African Rural Communities*, Cape Town: HSRC Press.

Nettleton, A., Charlton, J. and Rankin-Smith, F. (2003) *Engaging Modernities: Transformations of the Commonplace*, Johannesburg: University of the Witwatersrand Art Galleries.

Nettleton, A., Charlton, J. and Rankin-Smith, F. (eds) (2004) *Voice-Overs: Wits Writings Exploring African Artworks*, Johannesburg: University of the Witwatersrand Art Galleries.

New London Group (1996) 'A Pedagogy of Multiliteracies: designing social futures', *Harvard Educational Review* 66 (1): 60–92.

Newfield, D. and Stein, P. (2000) 'The Multiliteracies Project: South African Teachers Respond', in B. Cope and M. Kalantzis (eds) *Multiliteracies: Literacy Learning and the Design of Social Futures*, London and New York: Routledge.

Newfield, D. and Maungedzo, R. (2006) 'Mobilising and Modalising Poetry in a Soweto Classroom', *English Studies in Africa* 49 (1): 71–94.

Newfield, D., Andrew, D., Stein, P. and Maungedzo, R. (2003) "No number can describe how good it was": assessment issues in the multimodal classroom', *Assessment in Education* 10 (1): 61–81.

Norris, S. (2004) *Analysing Multimodal Interaction: a Methodological Framework*, New York and London: Routledge.

Norton, B. and Tooney, K. (2004) (eds) *Critical Pedagogies and Language Learning*, Cambridge: Cambridge University Press.

Nuttall, S. (ed.) (2006) *Beautiful Ugly: Africa and Diaspora Aesthetics*, Durham and London: Duke University Press.

O'Halloran, K. (2000) 'Classroom discourse in mathmatics: a multi-semiotic analysis'. *Linguistics and Education* 10(3): 359–88.

O'Halloran, K. (ed.) (2004) *Multimodal Discourse Analysis*, London: Continuum.

Oleson, V.L. (2000) 'Feminisms and Qualitative Research at and into the Millenium', in N.K. Denzin and Y.S. Lincoln (eds) *Handbook of Qualitative Research*, 2nd edn, London: Thousand Oaks; New Delhi: Sage Publications.

Olsen, D. (1996) *The World on Paper: the Conceptual and Cognitive Implications of Writing and Reading*, Cambridge: Cambridge University Press.

Ong, W. J. (1982) *Orality and Literacy: the Technologising of the Word*, London: Metheun.

Opland, J. (1983) *Xhosa Oral Poetry: Aspects of a Black South African Tradition*, Johannesburg: Ravan Press.

Ormerod, F. and Ivanic, R. (2002) 'Materiality in children's meaning-making practices', in *Visual Communication* 1 (1): 65–91.

Pahl, K. (2003) 'Children's text making at home: transforming meaning across modes', in C. Jewitt and G. Kress (eds) *Multimodal Literacy*, New York: Peter Lang.

Pahl, K. and Rowsell, J. (2005) *Literacy and Education: Understanding New Literacy Studies in the Classroom*, London: Sage.

Pahl, K. and Rowsell, J. (eds) (2006) *Travel Notes from the New Literacy Studies: Instances of Practice*, Clevedon: Multilingual Matters.

Phelan, P. (1993) *Unmarked: the Politics of Performance*, London and New York: Routledge.

Plato (1995) *Phaedrus*, trans. A. Nehamas and P. Woodruff, Indianapolis, IN: Hackett Publishing Co.

Prinsloo, M. (2004) 'Literacy is child's play: making sense in Kwezi Park', *Language and Education* 18 (4): 291–304.

Prinsloo, M. and Breier, M. (eds) (1996) *The Social Uses of Literacy: Theory and Practice in Contemporary South Africa*, Amsterdam: John Benjamins; Cape Town: SACHED Books.

Prinsloo, M. and Stein, P. (2005) "Down, Up and Round": Setting Children up as Readers and Writers in South African Classrooms', in J. Anderson, M. Kendrick, T. Rogers and S. Smythe (eds) *Portraits of Literacy across Families, Communities and Schools: Intersections and Tensions*, Mahwah, NJ and London: Lawrence Erlbaum Associates.

Reynolds, P. (1989) *Childhood in Crossroads: Cognition and Society in South Africa*, Cape Town and Johannesburg: David Philip.

Rock, B. (ed.) (1997) *Spirals of Suffering*, Pretoria: Human Sciences Research Council Publishers.

Rogoff, B. (2003) *The Cultural Nature of Human Development*, Oxford: Oxford University Press.

Rosen, H. (1984) *Stories and Meanings*, Sheffield: National Association for the Teaching of English.

Saussure, F. de (1974) *Course in General Linguistics*, ed. J. Culler, trans. W. Baskin, London: Fontana.

Scheub, H. (1975) *The Xhosa Intsomi*, Oxford: Clarendon Press.

Scribner, S. and Cole, M. (1981) *The Psychology of Literacy*, Cambridge, MA: Harvard University Press.

Seedat, M., Duncan, N. and Lazarus, S. (2001) *Community Psychology: Theory, Method and Practice*, New York: Oxford University Press.

Sen, A. (2006) *Identity and Violence: the Illusion of Destiny*, London: Allen Lane.

Seremetakis, C.N. (1994) 'The Memory of the Senses, Part 1: Marks of the Transitory', in C.N. Seremetakis (ed.) *The Senses Still: Perception and Memory as Material Culture in Modernity*, Chicago, IL: University of Chicago Press.

Shortis, T. and Jewitt, C. (2005) 'A "multimodal ecology of text" in Advanced Level English Language examinations?' *English in Education* 39 (2): 76–96.

Sideris, T. (2004) 'Borsh Maziba and The Long Walk to Freedom: The Diary of an Abused and Neglected Boy as a "Transitional Space" – Implication for Therapeutic Practice', unpublished paper, Wits Institute of Economic and Social Research, University of the Witwatersrand.

Smagorinsky, P., Zoss, M. and O'Donnell-Allen, C. (2005) 'Mask-making as identity project in a high school English class: a case study; *English in Education* 39 (2): 60–75.

Small, C. (1998) '*Musiking: The Meanings of Performance and Listening*', Hanover, NH: Wesleyan University Press.

Sontag, S. (1977) *On Photography*, London: Penguin Books.

Stein, P. (1993) 'For a Brighter Future: SPEAK Project in Soweto', in D. McKeon and K.D. Samway (eds) *Common Threads of Practice: Teaching English to Children Around the World*, Alexandria, VA: TESOL.

Stein, P. (1998) 'Reconfiguring the past and the present: performing literacy histories in a Johannesburg classroom', *TESOL Quarterly* 32 (3): 517–28.

Stein, P. (2000) 'Teaching Issues: rethinking resources: multimodal pedagogies in the ESL classroom', *TESOL Quarterly* 34 (2): 333–6.

Stein, P. (2001) 'Classrooms as Sites of Textual, Cultural and Linguistic Re-appropriation' in B. Comber and A. Simpson (eds) *Negotiating Critical Literacy in Classrooms*, Mahwah, NJ and London: Lawrence Erlbaum.

Stein, P. (2003) 'The Olifantsvlei "Fresh Stories" Project: Multimodality, Creativity and Fixing in the Semiotic Chain', in Jewitt, C. and Kress, G. (eds) *Multimodal Literacy*, New York: Peter Lang.

Stein, P. (2004) 'Representation, Rights and Resources: Multimodal Pedagogies in the Language and Literacy Classroom', in B. Norton and K. Toohey (eds) *Critical Pedagogies and Language Learning*, Cambridge: Cambridge University Press.

Stein, P. (2006) 'Fresh Stories', in S. Nuttall (ed.), *Beautiful Ugly: African and Diaspora Aesthetics*, Durham and London: Duke University Press.

Stein, P. (2007) 'Multimodal Instructional Practices', in D. Leu, J. Coiro, M. Knobel and C. Lankshear, (eds) *Handbook of Research on New Literacies*, Mahwah, NJ: Lawrence Erlbaum Associates.

Stein, P. and Newfield, D. (2006) 'Multiliteracies and multimodality in English in education in Africa: mapping the terrain', *English Studies in Africa* 49 (1): 1–22.

Stein, P. and Slonimsky, L. (2006) 'Multimodal Literacy in Three Johannesburg Families', in K. Pahl and J. Rowsell (eds) *Travel Notes from the New Literacy Studies: Instances of Practice*, Clevedon: Multilingual Matters.

Straker, J. and Moosa, F. (1994) 'Interacting with trauma survivors in contexts of continuing trauma', *Journal of Traumatic Stress* 7: 1–9.

Street, B. (1984) *Literacy in Theory and Practice*, Cambridge: Cambridge University Press.

Street, B. (ed.) (1993) *Cross-cultural Approaches to Literacy*, Cambridge: Cambridge University Press.

Street, B. (1995) *Social Literacies: Critical Perspectives on Literacy in Development, Ethnography and Education*, London: Longman.

Street, B. (2000) 'Literacy events and literacy practices: theory and practice in the New Literacy Studies', in M. Martin-Jones and K. Jones (eds) *Multilingual Literacies: Reading and Writing Different Worlds*, Amsterdam: John Benjamins Publishing Company.

Street, B. (ed.) (2001) *Literacy and Development*, London and New York: Routledge.

Street, B. (ed.) (2005) *Literacies Across Educational Contexts: Mediating Learning and Teaching*, Philadelphia, PA: Caslon Publishing.

Taylor, C. (1992) '*Multiculturalism and "The Politics of Recognition"*', in A. Guttman (ed.) *Multiculturalism*, Princeton, NJ: Princeton University Press.

Taylor, N. and Vinjevold, P. (1999) (eds) *Getting Learning Right: Report of the President's Education Initiative Research Project*, Johannesburg: Joint Education Thrust.

Thesen, L. and van Pletzen, E. (2006) (eds) *Academic Literacy and the Languages of Change*, London and New York: Continuum.

United Kingdom Literacy Association/Qualifications and Curriculum Authority (2004) *More Than Words: Multimodal Texts in the Classroom*, London: QCA, www.qca.org.uk/9054.html.

United Kingdom Literacy Association/Qualifications and Curriculum Authority (2005) *More Than Words 2: Creating Stories on Page and Screen*, London: QCA, www.qca.org.uk/15953.html.

Van Leeuwen, T. (1999) *Speech, Music, Sound*, London: Macmillan.

Van Leeuwen, T. (2000) 'It was just like Magic – a multimodal analysis of children's writing', *Linguistics and Education* 10 (3): 273–305.

Van Leeuwen, T. (2005) *Introducing Social Semiotics*, London and New York: Routledge.

Varenne, H. and McDermott, R. (1998) *Successful Failure: the School America Builds*, Boulder, CO: Westview Press.

Voloshinov, V.N. (1973) *Marxism and the Philosophy of Language*, New York: Seminar Press.

Voloshinov, V.N. (1986 [1929]) *Marxism and the Philosophy of Language*, Cambridge, MA: Harvard University Press.

Vygotsky, L.S. (1978) *Mind in Society – the Development of Higher Psychological Processes*, eds M. Cole, V. John-Steiner, S. Scribner and E. Souberman, Cambridge, MA: Harvard University Press.

Vygotsky, L.S. (1986) *Thought and Language*, ed. and trans. A. Kozulin, Cambridge, MA: MIT Press.

Wells, G. (1987) *The Meaning Makers: Children Learning Language and Using Language to Learn*, London: Hodder and Stoughton.

Wemmer, K. and Drew, M (2004) 'Designing think trails: using multiliteracies pedagogy to reshape academic knowledge into clinical reasoning', unpublished paper, Department of Audiology, University of the Witwatersrand, Johannesburg.

Wenger, E. (1998) *Communities of Practice: Learning, Meaning and Identity*, Cambridge, MA: Harvard University Press.

Wertsch, J.V. (1985) *Vygotsky and the Social Formation of Mind*, Cambridge, MA and London: Harvard University Press.

Winnicott, D. (1958) *Collected Papers. Through Paediatrics to Psycho-Analysis,* New York: Basic Books, Inc.

Wolpe, A., Quinlan, O. and Martinez, L. (1997) 'Gender Equity in Education', report by the Gender Equity Task team, Dept. of Education, South Africa.

Wood, K. and Jewkes, R. (1998) 'Love is a dangerous thing: micro-dynamics of violence in sexual relationships of young people in Umtata', Pretoria: CERSA – Women's Health Medical Research Council.

Wood, K., Maforah, F. and Jewkes, R. (1996) 'Sex, violence and constructions of love among Xhosa adolescents: putting violence on the sexuality education agenda', Tygerberg, Cape Town: CERSA – Women's Health Medical Research Council.

Wyatt-Smith, C. and Kimber, K. (2005) 'Valuing and evaluating student-generated online multimodal texts: rethinking what counts', *English in Education* 39 (2): 22–44.

Young, I. (1997) 'Difference as a Resource for Democratic Communication', in J. Bohman and W. Rehg (eds) *Democracy: Essays on Reason and Politics*, Cambridge MA: MIT Press.

# Index

Note: page numbers in **bold type** refer to illustrations.

## A library at your fingertips!

eBooks are electronic versions of printed books. You can store them on your PC/laptop or browse them online.

They have advantages for anyone needing rapid access to a wide variety of published, copyright information.

eBooks can help your research by enabling you to bookmark chapters, annotate text and use instant searches to find specific words or phrases. Several eBook files would fit on even a small laptop or PDA.

**NEW:** Save money by eSubscribing: cheap, online access to any eBook for as long as you need it.

### Annual subscription packages

We now offer special low-cost bulk subscriptions to packages of eBooks in certain subject areas. These are available to libraries or to individuals.

For more information please contact webmaster.ebooks@tandf.co.uk

We're continually developing the eBook concept, so keep up to date by visiting the website.

**www.eBookstore.tandf.co.uk**

Made in the USA
Middletown, DE
30 August 2017